LEGAL WRITING

FOR INTERNATIONAL STUDENTS

LEGAL WRITING FOR INTERNATIONAL STUDENTS

A U.S. legal writing textbook for ESL/ESP students and
practitioners of law and business

Susan Reid

Peconic Press
2005

Copyright 2005 Susan Reid. Printed and bound in the USA. All rights reserved. No part of this book may be reproduced or transmitted in any form or by any means, electronic or mechanical, including photocopying, recording, or by an information storage and retrieval system, except for the purpose of a book review for a journal, newspaper, or on the Web, without permission in writing by the publisher. For information, please contact Peconic Press, info@peconicpress.com.

Although the author and publisher have made every effort to ensure the accuracy and completeness of information contained in this book, we assume no responsibility for errors, inaccuracies, omissions, or any inconsistency herein. This textbook does not provide legal advice and should not be used in place of consultation with an attorney as needed.

ISBN   0-9768176-0-8

LCCN 2005903515

ATTENTION UNIVERSITIES, LAW SCHOOLS, MBA PROGRAMS, CORPORATIONS, LAW FIRMS, AND PROFESSIONAL ORGANIZATIONS: Quantity discounts are available on bulk purchases of this book for educational, gift purposes, or as premiums for increasing journal subscriptions or renewals. Special books or book excerpts can also be created to meet specific purposes. For information, please contact Peconic Press, P.O. Box 370631, West Hartford, CT. 06137. Email: info@peconicpress.com

About the Author

The author holds degrees in Teaching English as a Second Language, Social Work, and Law and is a graduate of Cornell University and the University of Pennsylvania, as well as the University of Connecticut. She has had many years of teaching experience and curriculum design in the University of Pennsylvania's English Language Program and in Yale's English Language Institute Law Seminar. She has published numerous articles about teaching methodology and cross-cultural communication in counseling and teaching.

About the Publisher

Peconic Press (www.peconicpress.com) publishes works reflecting the values that support environmental protection and sustainable development. The following statement was submitted by the author to demonstrate this interrelationship :

```
    Legal Writing for International Students is offered
in recognition of the compelling need for clear and precise
international communication in the field of law and related
disciplines. The textbook supports sustainable development
through cross-cultural legal education and a commitment to
world-wide individual and international justice.
```

Acknowledgements

The author wishes to acknowledge for their support :

Dr. Jan Hortas, Director, English Language Institute (ELI), Yale University
Professor Jack Sahl, Director, ELI Law Seminar, Yale University
Dean Eric Gouvin, Western New England School of Law
Professor Eric Strasser, University of Connecticut School of Law
Professor Mark Janis, University of Connecticut School of Law
Dr. Mary Ann Julian, Associate Director, English Language Program, University of
Pennsylvania
The students of the Yale ELI Law Seminar 2001-2004, with special thanks to:

Fabian Martens, Switzerland
Dennis Leung, Hong Kong
Oxana Serivanova, Russia
Bahar Teksoy, Turkey
Ji Yeon Song, Korea
Guillermo Castorena, Mexico

LEGAL WRITING FOR INTERNATIONAL STUDENTS

A U.S. Legal Writing Textbook for ESL/ESP students and practitioners of law and business.

Susan Reid

Table of Contents

INTRODUCTION

I. Textbook Overview
II. Writing Requirements for J.D. and LLM Students in the U.S.

The following areas of writing requirements are explored in this textbook. It is important for students to be proficient in writing in many of the following skill areas before beginning their graduate degree program.

    A. Rhetorical Modes: Basic Essay Structure, Summary, Comparison, Persuasion
    B. Note-taking
    C. Paraphrasing
    D. Writing a case brief
    E. Writing a reaction and a report
    G. Writing business letters
    H. Writing in the "irac" format
    I. Writing a contract
    J. Writing a research paper/ journal article/ thesis

III. Writing Requirements for J.D. students and practicing attorneys in the U.S.

Please note that students are not presumed to be familiar with the following prior to attending law school and that these areas are not explored in this textbook.

    A. Appellate brief
    B. Office memo

IV. Writing with Citations-"Bluebooking"
V. Using Legal Contexts

VI. Self-Editing
VII. Reviewing Grammar

CHAPTER ONE-WRITING AN ESSAY

I. Overview of Sentence, Paragraph, and Essay Structure & Exercises

    A. Sentence structure
    B. Paragraph structure
        1. Topic sentences: paragraphs concluding or beginning with the topic sentence
        2. Coherence
    C. Essay structure
        1. The introduction of an essay
        2. The body of an essay
        3. Connectors between paragraphs
        4. The conclusion of an essay

    Essay Example A (structure)

II. Preparing to write an essay: topic, audience, outline & Exercises

CHAPTER ONE- Grammar Review & Exercises

Perfect tenses
Passive voice
Tenses in if-sentences
Sentence punctuation review: period, semi-colon, colon, quotation marks, comma

    <u>Chapter One Legal Contexts:</u>
        Torts (negligence: foreseeability)

CHAPTER TWO-WRITING A SUMMARY

I. Overview
II. Reading Strategies
III. Vocabulary Building Strategies
IV. Paraphrasing & Exercises
V. Structures with "but for" & Exercises
VI. Writing a Summary & Exercises
VII. Writing an Abstract & Exercises
VIII. Writing a Case Brief & Exercises

CHAPTER TWO-Grammar Review & Exercises

Essential and Non-essential Relative Clauses
Punctuation of Essential and Non-essential Relative Clauses

> **Chapter Two Legal Contexts:**
> Environmental law, Health law, Constitutional law (First Amendment), Torts (negligence: but for), Corporate law

CHAPTER THREE-WRITING A REPORT & WRITING A REACTION

I. Writing a Report & Exercises
II. Writing a Reaction & Exercises

    Essay Example B (reaction)

III. Reading: U.S. Supreme Court and Equal Protection & Exercises
IV. Reading: Legal Theory & Exercises

CHAPTER THREE-Grammar Review & Exercises

Subject-verb inversion

    Chapter Three Legal Contexts:
        Legal Theory (positivism), Corporate Law,
        Constitutional law (role of U.S. Supreme Court, equal protection, capital punishment)

CHAPTER FOUR-WRITING A COMPARISON

I. Outlining a Comparison

    A. Comparing items
    B. Comparing points

    Essay Example C (comparison)

II. Reading- two cases in international law
III. Reading-Jurisdiction in international law

CHAPTER FOUR- Grammar Review & Exercises

Parallel structure
Subject-verb agreement

    <u>Chapter Four Legal Contexts:</u>
        International law, Constitutional law (treaties), Civil and Criminal Procedure (jurisdiction)

CHAPTER FIVE-WRITING TO PERSUADE

Guidelines for Writing to Persuade

> Essay Examples A and D (persuasion)

CHAPTER FIVE-Grammar Review & Exercises

Phrasal verbs

> **Chapter Five Legal Contexts:**
> Intellectual Property, International law (capital punishment)

CHAPTER SIX-WRITING BUSINESS LETTERS

I. Overview
II. Format/ Titles
III. Greetings
IV. Beginning
V. Middle
VI. Pre-Closing
VII. Closing
VIII. Examples of Business Letters & Exercises

CHAPTER SIX-Grammar Review & Exercises

Verbs plus gerunds or infinitives
Like/ As

Reading- Corporate Law

> **Chapter Six Legal Contexts:**
> Torts (defamation), Employment law,
> Professional Responsibility (scope of representation letters)
> Corporate law

CHAPTER SEVEN- WRITING IN THE IRAC FORMAT

I. Overview
II. Use of "irac" by law students
III. IRAC

    A. Introduction
    B. Issue identification
    C. Issue statement
    D. Rule statement
    E. Application
    F. Conclusion

CHAPTER SEVEN-Grammar Review & Exercises

Participles as adjectives-past, present, "dangling"

    <u>Chapter Seven Legal Context:</u>
        Torts (negligence)

CHAPTER EIGHT-WRITING A CONTRACT

I. Introduction
II. Content of a contract & Exercises
III. Language of a contract & Exercises

    A. Importance of language
    B. General language
    C. Specific language
    D. Additional contract vocabulary

IV. Reading a contract & Exercises

    A. Reading a contract to note language and structure
    B. Reading a contract for content
    C. Reading a contract in order to advise a client
    D. Reading to practice comprehension/paraphrasing
    E. Additional reading practice

CHAPTER EIGHT- Grammar Review & Exercises

Articles

    <u>Chapter ight Legal Contexts:</u>

Contracts: construction, sale of personal property,
employment (physician and hospital), copyright
Worker's Compensation laws

CHAPTER NINE-WRITING A RESEARCH PAPER

I. Introduction
II. Usage of the term "research" in law
III. Research skills
IV. Information Gathering
V. Writing an Outline
VI. Preparation of citations
VII. Final Outline
VIII. Writing the First Draft & Exercises
    A. Focus
    B. Synthesis
        1. introductory phrases
        2. verbs used to report information

Essay Example C (synthesis)

CHAPTER NINE-Grammar Review & Exercises

Avoidance of first and second persons
Articles and Quantifiers

> Chapter Nine Legal Contexts:
> Criminal law

CHAPTER TEN-EDITING

I. Grammar/Writing/Editing Activity: interpreting quotations

II. Discussion/Writing/Editing Activity: "the right to bear arms"

III. Discussion-instructor's corrections

IV. Student presentation of a grammar activity

V. Editing practice-punctuation

VI. Editing practice-grammar

Essay Example D (persuasion) (editing exercise)

CHAPTER TEN-Reference Information

Self-Editing in Academic Writing Checklist-usages to avoid

Correction Symbols

Websites for Students and Attorneys

Connectors-logical and sequential

Verbs and Adjectives plus Prepositions

Phrasal Verbs and Possible Synonyms

Verbs plus Gerunds or Infinitives

Irregular Verbs

> **Chapter Ten Legal Context:**
> **Constitutional law (Bill of Rights)**

END NOTES

LEGAL WRITING FOR INTERNATIONAL STUDENTS

A U.S. legal writing textbook for ESL/ESP students and practitioners of law and business.

INTRODUCTION

I. Textbook Overview

Write something worth reading or do something worth writing.
Benjamin Franklin 1.

The textbook is offered for use by all international students and practitioners of law for whom English is not a native language, and who intend to study in the U.S., to practice in the U.S., or to conduct business or legal transactions with U.S. corporations and law firms. While the academic focus of the textbook is based on the writing needs of pre-LLM students, the textbook is also appropriate for use in supplementary writing classes for pre-MBA students and for other advanced ESL students who plan to study in the U.S.

The goal of the textbook's methodology is independence, preparing students to be able to edit their own writing. The textbook may serve as a reference for independent study to be used by lawyers or law students. It may also serve as the primary textbook for advanced English as a Second Language (ESL) and English for Specific Purposes (ESP) classes for lawyers and law students or as a supplemental writing textbook for all advanced ESL students who are interested in improving their academic writing skills, while practicing legal writing formats and legal contexts.

The textbook is modular in design, and each unit offers the opportunity to practice writing essays in a particular rhetorical mode that is generic to all disciplines, using legal contexts. The modules also include instruction and exercises in writing business letters and reports, and the content of these modules may also be directly applicable to other professions, in particular the field of business administration, as well as law. Review exercises for key areas of advanced grammar are also provided.

Moreover, the modules address the major forms of legal writing that are taught in J.D. and LLM programs in the U.S. and that are practiced by U.S. attorneys. Those that are most frequently and widely used are explored in depth, with exercises offering opportunities to practice these forms of legal writing.

II. Writing requirements for JD and LLM students in the U.S.

Law school in the U.S. prepares students for the Juris Doctor degree. The J.D. degree is required for the practice of law in the U.S. Law students in the U.S. are graduate students; that is, they have already completed a Bachelor's degree. Completing a J.D. program generally requires three years of full-time study.

Students from the U.S. who hold a J.D. degree may apply to LLM programs in order to specialize, although an LLM degree is not required by most employers. International students who have completed an undergraduate or graduate degree in law in their countries often find that an LLM degree is an asset to their future plans. Therefore, a high percentage of international students in most LLM programs in U.S. law schools are international students.

All graduates of law schools in the U.S. or any other country who wish to practice law in the U.S. must pass a Bar exam. At the present time, New York is the only state that allows law school graduates who are not permanent residents of the U.S. to take its Bar exam.

The following areas of writing requirements are explored in this textbook. With the exceptions of writing a case brief and writing in the "irac" format, students will need to be capable of writing in the following skill areas before beginning their graduate degree program.

A. Rhetorical modes of essay writing-The rhetorical modes that are most necessary for law students and lawyers include narratives, summaries, persuasive writing (argumentation), reactions, comparisons, and reports. In a research paper or journal article, these modes are often used in a variety of combinations chosen by the writer. Moreover, some of the modes overlap with each other. For example, while a narrative is usually a description of a personal observation or experience, a report is a more objective presentation of facts. A reaction contains a summary of an objective description with a personal opinion. While subjective and objective descriptions cannot always be separated, narratives, reports, and reactions are closely intertwined. Moreover, a reaction may be written persuasively, or it may include a comparison with another writer's comments.

B. Note-taking -In addition, for law students in both JD and LLM programs, note-taking skills are essential, as in all University classes. Students generally develop their own system of abbreviations for note-taking of class lectures and discussions, but it is imperative for non-native speakers to be able to "think in English" and to take notes quickly in English. There is not time during a lecture to translate a professor's statements and to take notes in your first language. Students may request permission from professors to tape record classes.

Knowing the purpose for which the notes will be used will ensure more efficient and useful note-taking. For example, will the course include a quiz or an exam? Will the content of the lecture be important to your chosen topic for a research paper? Is it important to know the content for future class discussions? Is it important to know just the main ideas or to have a more detailed familiarity with some or all of the content?

For note-taking of reading, students again need to determine the purpose of the reading. Is the reading from a library book that might be useful for citing in a research paper? In that case, you would need to take notes only on those segments of the reading that you might find useful for your project.

Will there be a general class discussion about the reading? If so, you might want to note points that you would like to raise or to question. Does the professor call on students in class in reference to the reading assignments? If so, what are they generally expected to know about the reading?

If you are assigned to read one or more cases, you might want to brief the cases. If you are called on in a law class to tell about a case, you will be expected to tell the procedural history of the case, the facts, the issue, the holding, and possibly the court's reasoning.

With a few exceptions for famous cases, it is not necessary to memorize your briefs of cases you have read to prepare for an exam. However, it will be important on exams to know how to apply a given precedent to a hypothetical issue and set of facts. You will also be expected to know the major rules of case law, such as causation in torts. Your class notes on lectures and discussions will be especially useful here.

C. Paraphrasing-While paraphrasing another writer's main ideas is a key element of writing a summary, law students and lawyers must also become proficient in the ability to paraphrase every part of a writer's statements, that is, to paraphrase sentences, not just main ideas. This is especially important when reading and interpreting statutes or when reading and interpreting contracts.

D. Writing a case brief- While students will need to know in advance how to write a summary, having experience with summarizing a case is not necessary upon entry into a law school degree program. Writing a case brief (briefing a case) is a skill that is important to both law students and lawyers. A case brief usually includes a summary of the facts of the case, the procedural history (the courts that previously heard the case and their holdings), the holding of the case at hand, and one or more sentences about the reasoning of the court. The format of a case brief is somewhat flexible and depends on the purpose for which the brief is being written.

E. Writing a reaction- Writing reactions to all or part of a reading assignment is often required in elective seminars in JD and LLM programs. Sometimes students are asked to write a persuasive reaction. Students may also be asked to post their reactions on the seminar group mailing list for all students to read prior to a class discussion.

F. Writing in the "irac" format- Students are not presumed to be familiar with writing in this format prior to attending law school. However, for international students, it is advisable, before beginning a JD or LLM program, to become aware of the case law (common law) system on which "irac" is based, as well as the role of lawyers in common law, by knowing the basic structure and purpose of "irac" writing.

N.B. The U.S. common law legal system includes not only case law, but also statutes, as well as other codes, including the Federal Rules of Civil Procedure and the Federal Rules of Evidence. You may find these and other codes on the Legal Information Institute website.

G. Writing a research paper/journal article/thesis- Some courses in JD and LLM programs require writing a final research paper. Others offer students a choice between taking a final examination and writing a research paper. Often law student research papers are required to be of nearly publishable quality, and as such, represent the style and format of a law journal article. Some LLM programs require students to complete a thesis, which entails the same writing skills as those needed to write a research paper.

III. Additional writing requirements for JD students and practicing attorneys

Please note that neither of the following areas of legal writing is explored in this textbook. Moreover, students are not expected to be familiar with them prior to attending law school.

A. Appellate brief-This form of legal brief writing involves using the "irac" format to persuade a judge. An appellate brief refers to cases on appeal and are presented in conjunction with oral arguments. Sometimes the same case precedent is used by both the prosecuting and defense attorneys in their appellate briefs to persuade a judge as to the most advisable outcome of a case. Lawyers also choose other case rules to make their position as strong as possible. Writing an appellate brief is required in JD programs where Moot Court is a required course for JD students. Writing an appellate brief, however, is usually optional for LLM students.

B. Office memo- This form of legal writing involves using the "irac" format to foresee the possible outcomes of a case that has been presented by a prospective client for a supervising attorney who will need to decide whether to accept that case. The research of case precedents involved in writing an office memo is similar to that needed to prepare an appellate brief; however, a memo is written to predict, rather than to persuade. Knowing how to write an office memo is required for J.D. students and practicing attorneys. Many law schools also require LLM students to take one semester of legal writing in which writing an office memo is included.

IV. Writing with citations

"Bluebooking"- Citations enable a writer to acknowledge other writers whose work is either quoted directly or paraphrased and discussed in the first writer's work, as well as to offer reference information so that readers may look up in their entirety the works that are cited. There are also formats for referencing cases and statutes.

The legal profession in the U.S. uses its own citation format. The citation system for the law profession is catalogued in a reference book entitled, <u>The Bluebook: a Uniform System of Citation</u> (" Bluebook") 2., which law students and practitioners need to use on a regular basis. J.D. and LLM students are not expected to be familiar with this system before beginning a law degree program. However, it might be useful to purchase a copy of the "Bluebook" in advance and to review the purpose and organization of the book before starting classes. You will also need to use the "Bluebook" if you plan to publish a law journal article in the U.S.

V. Using legal contexts

While this textbook provides a sampling of legal contexts in which to practice the forms of writing required for U.S. lawyers, the textbook is not intended to be "content-based". That is, although information related to a broad variety of fields of law will be provided as a basis for writing practice, such legal information is not intended to be comprehensive, and many important areas of law are not included in the contexts.

VI. Self-editing

In addition to offering legal contexts with the goal of developing academic and legal writing skills in English, the textbook also intends for students to become more independent and skillful as editors of their own writing. An editing system using correction symbols for each of a variety of frequent errors in academic writing at the advanced level is provided in Chapter Ten. Instructors and students may choose to refer to this system or to develop an editing system of their own.

This system allows instructors to indicate with symbols where students have made errors in essays written for class assignments. Each symbol shows to which area of grammar or structure the error relates, but teachers do not complete the actual corrections. Students then determine how the sentence must be rewritten in order to correct the error. Using such a system encourages students to develop self-editing skills. The long-range goal is for students eventually to identify and correct a majority of their own errors when they proofread their work, that is, to develop the ability to self-edit in English.

Instructors complete the correction chart and return it to students after reading each submitted assignment. Both instructors and students keep a master record of the form, which can then become a useful way to determine in which areas students are making the most errors.

Students are encouraged to raise questions in class about the instructor's corrections and other editing suggestions which may be unclear and even to disagree with the instructor about the editing. Instructors may need to remind and encourage students to ask for explanations in class or to make an appointment with the instructor to discuss their writing in more detail. Also, depending on the needs of the students as a whole, instructors may choose to present additional exercises in the grammar of the corrected areas in class.

The important value of independence in the U.S. relates to many arenas of life, including to the academic setting. Graduate students, especially, are expected to set their own goals and to take responsibility for their own learning, which includes asking for clarification or advice when needed from all instructors and to voice their opinions, even when they differ from those of the instructors.

Moreover, from a linguistic standpoint, it is more useful to the learning process for students to receive feedback that identifies possible errors or a need for revision, but does not include specific corrections. When students note the errors indicated by the instructor and then are asked to make the corrections themselves (or to raise questions if they do not find an error), they are more likely to avoid making the same error in future writing than if the instructor corrects the errors. By playing a more active role in the editing process, students will learn more from their writing errors and progress more rapidly towards greater independence in writing.

VII. Reviewing grammar

Each chapter of the textbook will present grammar and editing exercises related to the "Self-Editing in Academic Writing Checklist" found in Chapter Ten. These areas of editing incorporate the grammar areas that are generally reviewed in advanced grammar classes. Students are encouraged to raise additional questions about all areas of grammar in class. Students should refer to a grammar textbook if they need additional clarification. For further ideas for grammar review, please see Chapter Ten.

CHAPTER ONE

WRITING AN ESSAY

I. Overview of Sentence, Paragraph, and Essay Structure

    A. Sentence structure-

    Every sentence needs a subject and a verb. Not all combinations of words that have subjects and verbs (clauses) are complete sentences, however. An independent clause may stand alone as a complete sentence.

```
They sing.
```

A dependent clause contains a subject and verb, but may not stand alone because it is introduced by an adverb or a participle.

```
While they sing,

Hearing what they sing,
```

A sentence that contains a subject and a transitive verb may not stand alone without a direct object, unless the verb also has an intransitive meaning.

```
They sing a song.
They sing. (They know how to sing, or they participate in
singing.)

She holds (incomplete sentence)
She holds a law degree. (complete sentence)
```

A sentence that contains at least one independent and one dependent clause is called a complex sentence. Academic writing usually involves writing with complex sentences. At the same time, in English, most sentences have no more than two or possibly three clauses. More than three clauses would be considered a "run-on" sentence, or one too lengthy to be manageable in English.

B-1. Paragraph structure-topic sentence

Each paragraph in an essay should focus on one main idea. That main idea is found in the topic sentence of the paragraph, which is usually the first or last sentence.

Paragraph concluding with the topic sentence

The sentences in a paragraph that conclude with a topic sentence usually flow from the most general to the least general in meaning.

Many people prefer living in a large city. Urban employment opportunities, cultural and social activities, and convenient public transportation attract many residents. They may disparage life in a small town, especially one that is remote from all urban areas. There are, however, many advantages to living in a small town, including close-knit communities that assist each other in times of crisis, a low crime rate, and proximity to natural beauty. In fact, the advantages of living in a small town are often overlooked.

Paragraph beginning with the topic sentence

The subsequent sentences in a paragraph that begins with the topic sentence support the main idea.

The advantages of living in a small town are often overlooked. Living in a small town usually means experiencing a close-knit community whose members assist each other in times of crisis, a low crime rate, and proximity to natural beauty. While many people prefer living in a large city and even disparage small town life, residents of small towns continue to enjoy many features that city dwellers ignore.

Exercise B-1a:

In pairs or individually, write a paragraph that develops the following topic sentences.

a. The process of applying to a University involves several steps.

b. The Constitution of a country is generally based on several principles.

c. The internet has had a strong impact on communication in many ways.

d. Although lawyers vary greatly in their reasons for studying and practicing law, and many lawyers specialize in widely differing fields, all lawyers share similar professional values.

B-2. Paragraph structure-coherence

Connectors such as 'therefore', 'moreover', 'besides', 'in addition', at the beginning of sentences give a paragraph coherence by showing the interrelationship of the sentences:

There are, however, many advantages to living in a small town.

Other ways to link ideas to achieve paragraph coherence include the use of **repetition of key words or ideas** :

```
The advantages of living in a small town are often
overlooked. Living in a small town often means experiencing
close-knit communities.
```

The use of **pronouns and demonstrative adjectives** to refer to previously stated nouns also provides coherence:

```
Many people prefer living in a large city. They may
disparage life in a small town...

Small towns usually enjoy close-knit communities. This
means they may also enjoy a low crime rate.
```

Exercise B-2a:

In pairs or individually, practice using the suggested coherence strategies by writing a subsequent sentence for each of the following:

1. There are some areas of law that are considered transactional and do not generally involve litigation. (connector)

2. Lawyers are often asked to advise clients about whether to sign a contract. (repetition of key words)

3. "Clerking" for a judge provides excellent experience in case research. (pronoun)

4. Each state in the U.S. has its own requirements for joining the Bar Association. (repeated words)

Exercise B-2b:

The following passages lack coherence. Rewrite and/or reorder them till they form a coherent paragraph by using the above coherence strategies:

1. Copyright law must be reexamined in view of the challenges that the internet imposes. The internet has facilitated the exchange of written information. Recently, important changes have been made in international copyright law.

2. Patent law differs from copyright law. Patents and copyrights share many similarities. Patent lawyers usually have a background in science or engineering.

3. Criminal defense lawyers do not always believe in the innocence of their clients. All people should have the right to their day in court. Criminal defense lawyers, like all other lawyers, may not lie in court to protect their clients.

4. Tort law is an important area of law. Many people feel that tort claims are sometimes exaggerated. Many people feel that there should be a cap on the amount of damages that tort victims may receive.

Exercise B-2c:

In pairs or individually, while keeping the sentences in the same order, add logical connectors to the following paragraph to make it more cohesive:

If you want to practice law in the U.S., you must take a Bar examination. You must choose the state in the U.S. in which you would like to practice. Each state has somewhat different requirements. Many states offer the same multiple choice exam on the first day. The essay exam on the second day generally differs in each state. Some states have a three-day Bar exam. States vary in the minimum score that they require on the exam.

C. Essay structure

An essay is composed of at least three paragraphs: the introduction, body, and conclusion.

C1. The introduction of an essay

It is the custom in the U.S. to tell the reader as soon as possible the purpose of the essay. "Getting to the point" is highly valued in academic writing, and a reader should be able to identify readily the writer's purpose. Therefore, every essay should have a thesis statement that expresses the main idea of the essay as a whole. The thesis statement is found in the introductory paragraph or introductory section of the essay and is often either the first sentence of the essay or the last sentence of the introduction.

Moreover, a reader expects to learn the content of the essay by reading the introduction. A well-written introduction will contain a presentation of the general topic, a brief statement of the background of the topic that prompted the essay, and definitions of the primary issues and key terms, as well as the thesis statement.

Either of the following examples of paragraph structure that were introduced above could be used as an introductory paragraph for an essay entitled, "The Advantages of Living in a Small Town".

1a. Introductory paragraph ending with a topic sentence

The Advantages of Living in a Small Town

    Many people prefer living in a large city. Urban employment opportunities, cultural and social activities, and convenient public transportation attract many residents. They may disparage life in a small town, especially one that is remote from all urban areas. There are, however, many advantages to living in a small town, including close-knit communities that assist each other in times of crisis, a low crime rate, and proximity to natural beauty. In fact, the advantages of living in a small town are often overlooked.

1b. Introductory paragraph beginning with a topic sentence

The Advantages of Living in a Small Town

    The advantages of living in a small town are often overlooked. Living in a small town usually means experiencing a close-knit community whose members assist each other in times of crisis, a low crime rate, and proximity to natural beauty. While many people prefer living in a large city and even disparage small town life, residents of small towns continue to enjoy numerous features that city dwellers ignore.

    The information that the essay will provide may be specifically outlined in the introductory paragraph of an essay. For example, the following sentence could be added at the end of either of the above introductory paragraphs to complete the introduction for an essay.

    This essay will describe three important advantages to living in a small town.

C-2. The body of an essay

    The middle or body of an essay is composed of one or more paragraphs. Each body paragraph and its topic sentence support the thesis statement and develop the thesis in more detail. If the introduction states that the essay will discuss three advantages to living in a small town, for example, then there should be three body paragraphs, each describing one of the advantages.

C-3. Connectors between paragraphs

    Connectors between paragraphs are analogous to connectors between sentences in that they link ideas and provide coherence. Connectors that signal a transition between paragraphs often consist of a preposition plus a noun or gerund. Some connectors introduce additional ideas; others introduce an opposite idea in the subsequent paragraph.

    By visiting their neighbors regularly, small town residents usually form close-knit communities.

```
    While residents of small towns enjoy the support and friendship
of a close-knit community, they are also accustomed to a low crime rate
in their area.

    Not only is a close-knit community advantageous in times of
crisis, it may also contribute to a low crime rate in a given area.
```

C-4. The conclusion of an essay

A concluding paragraph or section is also required, however redundant its inclusion may seem. The conclusion restates the introduction in different words by summarizing the main points of the essay. The conclusion may also include the writer's final ideas about the topic at hand, including the writer's opinion, which may be presented as fact or as opinion, suggestions for further study, or other recommendations. However, the concluding paragraph does not introduce any additional ideas that have not already been discussed in the essay.

The second example of paragraph structure from B-1 above could be used as the concluding paragraph for an essay that began with the first example of paragraph structure in B-1.

Exercise E-1:

Here are some examples of thesis statements from the introduction of an essay. Write an appropriate concluding statement for the last paragraph of the essay.

1. The World Trade Organization requires all states who apply for membership to have a copyright infrastructure in place. This requirement, among other purposes, is intended to control international piracy.
    Therefore, _____

2. In countries that have civil law systems, judges rely more on statutes than on case precedents to make their decisions.
    Therefore, _____

3. In the U.S., a Supreme Court decision takes precedence over state law.
    It is clear that_____

4. International treaties often require signatories to develop implementing legislation.
    In brief, _____

Essay Example A (Structure)

The Advantages of Living in a Small Town

Many people prefer living in a large city. City dwellers may even disparage life in a small town, especially one that is remote from all urban areas. There are, however, many advantages to living in a small town, including convenience, close-knit communities, and proximity to recreational areas and natural beauty.

The first advantage to living in a small town is the convenience, primarily for doing daily errands. Small towns generally establish shopping areas within minutes by car of each residential area. These areas include ample parking spaces, allowing residents to complete a variety of errands, such as buying gas, taking clothes to the dry cleaner, and shopping for food and even gifts, without going to separate locations or spending time searching for parking.

Another advantage is the close-knit community of small town life. Neighbors in small towns usually introduce themselves and maintain frequent contact. In addition, they are likely to meet in other social, school, or business situations, thereby strengthening their ties. Close-knit communities tend to offer emotional support in times of stress or crisis. Small town residents do not move frequently, so these supportive friendships may continue for many years.

Finally, the proximity to recreational areas and natural beauty is an important advantage to living in a small town. Just as doing errands is not so time-consuming, going to the movies or to a sports event is convenient and does not usually involve waiting in line, waiting in traffic, or searching for a parking space. Residents of small towns also have places to enjoy nature, while hiking or bicycling, for example, within minutes of their homes.

In conclusion, life in a small town offers convenience for completing daily errands, a close-knit community, and proximity to recreational areas and natural beauty. While city dwellers may underestimate the benefits of small town life, residents of small towns continue to enjoy many advantages that city dwellers often overlook.

Exercise F-1:

Read the above example of an essay. What is the thesis of the essay? How does the essay fulfill its purpose as stated in the thesis? Is the essay based primarily on the author's opinion or does it appear to reflect facts? How does the author use connectors and other coherence strategies in the essay? Does the conclusion restate the introduction? Does the conclusion make any recommendations for further study? Does it add any new information other than opinion that was not presented earlier in the essay?

II. Preparing to write an essay: topic, audience, outline

Students, as well as practitioners, do not always have the luxury of choosing their own writing topic. Assigned writing topics are usually referred to as "prompts". When as a writer you do have the opportunity to write an essay on the topic of your choice, it is important to choose a topic that is narrow enough to manage thoroughly in an essay. In addition, it is important to remain focused on that topic throughout the writing process and to remove any information that does not relate directly to the essay prompt or to your purpose for writing, however interesting that information might be.

It is important to determine your intended audience for your essay before beginning to write. This will help you decide the general focus of your essay, as well as the information and explanations to include.

The first step in writing an outline is brainstorming. Think of all the concepts that you would like to include in the essay and write them in a list or diagram. Some writers find that drawing a diagram can show the inter-relationship of the concepts, the main and subordinate topics, and help determine the order in which to write about the main topics.

Next, when excerpts of the writing of other authors will be used, it is useful to make another list of all the ideas from readings with their citations that are relevant to the essay topic. The two lists may be combined by indicating to which sub-topic the ideas from the readings relate.

The final step is to write an outline of the main ideas of the essay, in the order in which the essay will address them. Ideas that will be incorporated from the readings or other reference material will be included in their appropriate places in the outline.

Writing the first draft of the essay means separating the outline into paragraphs. You may first choose to write the thesis statement for the essay and then a topic sentence for each paragraph before beginning the actual writing of each paragraph.

The process of choosing a topic and writing an outline is very similar for both the essay and research paper or journal article. We will return to these steps in the writing process as they relate to the research paper in a later chapter.

Exercise I-7:

Imagine that your audience is composed of lawyers and law students from a variety of countries. Write a thesis statement for an essay that will describe the legal system in your first country. Then write an outline or draw a diagram of the information that you would like to include. Next, write an introduction in one paragraph, stating three main characteristics of the legal system. Write a topic sentence for each of the body paragraphs, based on each of the three characteristics. Finally, write a 1-2 page essay about the legal system in your country with an introduction, conclusion, and three body paragraphs.

CHAPTER ONE-Grammar Review

Perfect tenses

Exercise I-1:

In pairs, write one sentence in each of the following tenses: present perfect, past perfect, future perfect. Then write one sentence in each of those tenses in the progressive form. Be prepared to read your sentences to the class and to explain the meaning of the tenses in your sentences.

Exercise I-2:

What is the difference in meaning between each of the following pairs of sentences? Be prepared to explain your answers to the class.

1. She has been teaching here for five years.
1. She taught here for five years.

2. He will call you then.
2. He will have called you then.

3. They began working at 8 A.M.
3. They had begun working at 8 A.M.

4. We enjoyed our visit to Italy when we went to Europe.
4. We have enjoyed our visit to Italy.

5. He wrote several books in his lifetime.
5. He has written several books.

Exercise I-3:

Answer the following true-false questions to show that you know the meaning of the tenses.

1. When I got home, my roommate left.
True or false: My roommate left and then I got home.

2. He will have graduated when he gets married.
True or false: His wedding will come before his graduation.

3. They had dinner when we got there.
True or false: They waited for us before having dinner.

4. I will have returned to the U.S. when you leave.
True or false: I will return before you leave.

5. They had studied for three hours when you called.
True or false: After you called, they studied for three hours.

Passive voice

All passive verbs are formed with "be" and "get" plus the past participle. The passive voice may be used in any verb tense.

However, since the progressive forms of the verb are informal, they are not generally used in academic writing. Moreover, since "get" is considered informal, it is not used in academic writing.

Please see Chapter Ten for a list of the most common irregular verbs, including past participles, in English.

N.B. While the passive voice is important in academic writing, it is not always advisable to use it in legal writing. For clarity, lawyers often need to express the agent as the subject of a sentence. In persuasive writing, lawyers usually avoid the passive voice because of the potentially greater impact of an active sentence. However, in a law journal article or research paper, writers might choose to use the passive voice as often as they would in other academic fields.

A. The passive is often used instead of the active when:

1. ... the writer wants to focus on the receiver of the action. The grammatical structure allows us to make the receiver the subject of the sentence, instead of the object. The agent of the action may be omitted in the passive voice or may be expressed in a prepositional phrase beginning with "by".

> **Active:** The First Amendment does not protect all forms of speech.
> **Passive:** Not all forms of speech are protected by the First Amendment. (All forms of speech are not protected by the First Amendment.)

2. ...the agent is less important to the meaning or emphasis of the sentence than the receiver, when the receiver is obvious, or when the receiver is unknown.

Active: Many people read that newspaper.
Passive: That newspaper is widely read.

Active: The University requires students to register in advance.
Passive: Students are required to register in advance.

Active: People who are native speakers of English consider the verb "to get" to be informal.
Passive: The verb "to get" is considered to be informal.

Active: Something has polluted the water supply of that town.
Passive: The water supply of that town has been polluted.

Exercise I-4:

Write an example of a passive sentence in every tense except the progressive tenses. Be prepared to discuss in pairs or as a group the purpose of the passive as compared with the active voice in each of your sentences.

B. Complex passives

Complex passives refer to sentences in the passive voice that include infinitives or are followed by "that-clauses". These structures are generally not used in informal conversation, but are frequently used in lectures and news reports. They are widely used in academic writing.

Examples:

It was reported that many residents were forced to flee the area.

Many residents were reported to have been forced to flee the area.

Exercise I-5:

Write a sentence with a complex passive that begins with each of the following passive structures. Then write a second sentence beginning with the unexpressed subject of the previous sentence and an infinitive structure.

Example:

a. It is expected that all assignments will be completed on time.
b. The professor expects all assignments to be completed on time.

1. It should be noted that
2. It is assumed that
3. It has been ruled that
4. It is alleged that
5. It is expected that

Tenses in If-Sentences-

There are several combinations of tenses that are possible with if-sentences, depending on the meaning of the conditional that they express. The following examples represent the most frequent usages of if-sentences.

```
present/present: If it rains, I take my umbrella.
Meaning-Whenever it rains, I always take my umbrella.

present/future: If it rains, I will take my umbrella.
Meaning-If it rains at a specified time, tomorrow or on the day
of the picnic, for example, I will take my umbrella.

present/imperative: If it rains, take your umbrella.
Meaning-If it rains (on a specified date), the speaker asks that
you take your umbrella.

past/would(conditional tense): If it rained, I would take my
umbrella.
Meaning-Although it is possible that it will rain, it is not as
likely as in example #2.

N.B. When the verb "to be" is found in the past tense with "if",
"were" is used with all pronouns. If I were you, I would take my
umbrella.

past perfect/would have (conditional perfect tense): If it had
rained, I would have taken my umbrella.
Meaning-The picnic is over, and I didn't take my umbrella because
it wasn't raining.
N.B. This combination of tenses is sometimes known as an "unreal
conditional" because the picnic is over, so it is no longer
possible to take an umbrella to the picnic.

past/conditional perfect: If you were a meteorologist, you would
have reminded me to take my umbrella.
Meaning-The if-clause represents an ongoing conditional, that is,
you are still not a meteorologist, but the event that the
conditional affected is over.
Compare-If you had been home when I left for the picnic, you
would have reminded me to take my umbrella. This conditional
applies only to the time when I was leaving for the picnic.
```

N.B. 1. Questions-Present tense questions and conditional tense questions with if-sentences follow the same tense patterns as described above.
Present with if/present: Do you mind if I take my umbrella?
Past with if/conditional: Would you mind if I took my umbrella?

2. Should- "Should" is sometimes used in place of "if" in formal statements with future meaning. Sometimes this structure implies a reprimand, and sometimes it indicates an unlikely event. With this structure, following "should", the base form is used for the verb "to be":

    a. Should you fail to register on time, you will be charged an additional fee.
    b. Should you be absent again, you will not receive credit for the course.
    c. Should the flight be canceled, you will be informed of your options.

3. Present imperative (see above example): If it rains, the speaker asks that you take your umbrella.

Some verbs in English are followed by a clause beginning with "that", and in subjunctive fashion, the "s" is omitted in the third person singular present tense. These verbs order someone to do something and include: ask, recommend, require, insist, suggest. This structure is formal and more polite than a direct imperative or a statement with an infinitive structure ("to tell someone to do something").

Compare:
If it rains on the evening of the meeting, we ask that you leave your umbrellas at the main entrance.
We are asking you to leave your umbrellas at the main entrance.
Please leave your umbrellas at the main entrance.

We asked that he leave quietly through the side door.
We told him to leave quietly through the side door.

His parents asked that he finish his studies before getting married.
His parents asked that his studies be finished before he got married.(This passive structure with the subjunctive is even more formal and polite than the active subjunctive structure because it omits direct finger-pointing at the person being asked to do something.)
His parent told him to finish his studies before getting married.

4. In a formal if-sentence, if the verb in the non-if-clause is in the conditional perfect, the subject and "had" may be inverted in the if-clause, while omitting "if":

Had you come home sooner, you would not have been caught in the rain. (If you had come home sooner, you would not have been caught in the rain.)

```
You would not have gotten drenched had you taken your umbrella.
(You would not have gotten drenched if you had taken your
umbrella.)
```

Exercise I-5:

In pairs, discuss the following situation to which you have been assigned. Prepare a role play in which each speaker uses at least two if-sentences in a brief conversation about the following. If you prefer not to perform a role play, write at least two possible conditional sentences for each speaker in the situation.

1. You return with a coat to the dry cleaner. Explain to the business owner why you are returning the coat to be cleaned again, why you should not have been charged for the dry cleaning, and why it is in the business owner's best interests to do a better job.
2. You stayed late at work and are the only one in the office. You leave to get a drink of water in the hallway and lock yourself out of the office. You are not carrying any identification with you. Explain the situation to the security guard, who has never seen you before, and ask him to open the door to your office.
3. You missed an important exam and have made an appointment with your professor. Explain what happened, and try to obtain permission to arrange for a make-up exam.
4. You are in the airport of a city that you have never visited before. You have just arrived and are not able to locate your luggage. You go to the ticket counter of the airline that brought you to this city.

Exercise I-6:

In pairs or individually, read the following paragraph, which summarizes the facts of <u>Palsgraf v. Long Island Rail Road Co</u>. 162 N.E.99 (N.Y. 1928). Then write at least four if- sentences related to these facts:

Mrs. Palsgraf was a Long Island Rail Road passenger. While she was standing on the platform, waiting for her train, passengers were entering the train that was already in the station. A railroad employee hurried a passenger onto the train by pushing him, causing the passenger to drop a package. The package, which contained fireworks, exploded, and hit a metal scale on the platform. When the scales fell, Mrs. Palsgraf was injured. Was the Long Island Rail Road responsible for Mrs. Palsgraf's injuries?

Exercise I-7:

In pairs, write a sentence for each of the following verbs, followed by a noun clause beginning with "that": ask, suggest, recommend, require, insist.

Sentence Punctuation Review

A. Period

Use a period at the end of a complete sentence.

```
There are four elements of negligence in U.S. torts law.
```

B. Semi-colon

The use of a semi-colon is optional. However, if you choose to use a semi-colon, it can take the place only of a period, not of a comma. It is most commonly used to separate independent clauses that are closely related in meaning. Because they are so related, the second clause often begins with a logical connector such as "however", "moreover", "therefore".

```
There are four elements of negligence; however, he wrote
about only three of them on the exam.
```

C. Colon

The use of a colon is optional. It is used to replace phrases that introduce a list of examples (such as, for example, including). In informal writing, a hyphen is often used instead of a colon.

```
There are four elements of negligence in U.S. torts law:
duty of care, breach of duty, causation, harm.
```

D. Quotation marks

Use double quotation marks to surround direct quotations, that is, the exact words that someone wrote or said. Use quotation marks, also, to surround slang or colloquial phrases in a text of formal writing.

```
Although the juvenile stated that he was only "hanging
out", the officer detained him for disturbing the peace.
```

Use single quotation marks when a quotation is included within another direct quotation.

```
The professor told the students, "Today we will discuss
what foreseeability means in torts and what Judge Cardozo
meant when he said, 'The risk reasonably to be perceived
defines the duty to be obeyed' in his famous decision of
Palsgraf v. Long Island Railroad Co.".
```

Do not close the quotation marks at the end of a paragraph if you are quoting more than one paragraph consecutively.

E. Comma

1. Use a comma to separate words in a series.

   > First year law students are generally required to study Torts, Civil Procedure, and Constitutional Law, *inter alia*.

2. Use a comma to set off an apposition

   > My professor, who specializes in real estate law, just published a textbook.

3. Use a comma between two independent clauses that are joined by a conjunction.

   > We studied legal writing, and then we worked part-time for a judge.

4. Use commas to set off a non-essential clause. (Please see Chapter Three for a more detailed review of essential and non-essential clauses.)

   > Professor Smith, who teaches international law, will be the guest speaker.
   > The professor who teaches international law will be the guest speaker.

5. Use a comma after an introductory adverbial clause (a clause found at the beginning of a sentence).

   > Whenever we have time, our study group meets after lunch to review the reading.

6. Use a comma after an introductory participial clause. (Please see Chapter Seven for a more detailed review of introductory participles.)

   > Meeting for at least an hour each week, our study group is able to discuss many questions about the reading.

7. Use a comma to set off connectors.

   > In addition, we recommend that you study environmental law.

8. Use a comma before and after a direct quotation.

   > The employer said, "In order to work for this NGO, you will need to study environmental law."

   > "In order to work for this NGO, you will need to study environmental law," said the employer.

CHAPTER THREE

WRITING A SUMMARY

I. Overview

There are many purposes for writing a summary. As a law student, you may want to summarize important points in a reading assignment to prepare for a class discussion. In lecture classes, when you read cases for homework, you may want to identify the issue of the case, the procedural history (in which courts the case was heard), the past and present holdings, and possibly the court's reasoning. By writing a summary of these points, you will be better prepared if you are called on in class. Writing a summary of a case is called a briefing a case.

Often lawyers and law students write summaries of one or more ideas of another writer to include in a longer essay. The ideas of another writer may be used to support your ideas in persuasive writing. On the other hand, you might summarize opposing ideas in order to refute them or to show what you consider to be the flaws in that viewpoint. You may also choose to compare the ideas of two or more writers and then show which writer you feel has the better argument. Finally, you will also need to summarize another writer's ideas in order to write a report or a reaction.

While searching for such sources to cite in your own work, you may take notes in the form of a short summary of one or more ideas from an article or book. Later you can use these notes to determine whether to include particular sources in your essay or article.

The ability to write an effective summary depends in part on the ability to identify the key sentences or passages in a text that encompass the writer's main ideas. As we have noted, main ideas in a well-written essay are found in the thesis sentence and topic sentences of each paragraph. Finding the main ideas and their reasoning that are embedded in longer essays depends in part on reading strategies.

The more quickly you can read, as well as comprehend, another writer's meaning, the sooner you can determine the relevance of the writing to your purpose. If you decide to summarize another writer's ideas in an essay of your own, for example, your reading skills will help you find the most relevant points to cite and to summarize.

II. Reading strategies

Three reading strategies are essential to the lawyer, as well as other professionals and students whose work involves reading large amounts of complex material in a relatively short time. These strategies include predicting, skimming, and scanning.

Predicting improves reading comprehension. Before you begin reading, take a few minutes to glance over the title, subtitle, and section headings of the text to determine as much as possible what the text will discuss and what questions it might answer. If you are reading for the purpose of choosing sources related to your own writing project, predicting can help you determine whether the text will be useful at this point.

Skimming involves reading the first sentence of every paragraph or section, in addition to chapter headings and all headings in bold print. Read the introduction and conclusion of the passage, as well. While skimming, try to identify the writer's main ideas. Then you can read in more detail only those paragraphs or sections that relate to your purpose. If you are responsible for summarizing the entire text, skimming allows you to begin an outline of your summary. It can also increase your reading speed when you return to read the text in more detail.

Scanning is often used in conjunction with skimming. Scanning means reading vertically through a text to find specific information. Identify the paragraphs or sections that most probably contain the information you need and then look quickly through them vertically, seeking key relevant words. If you have a list of assigned questions or your own questions related to your search for sources, scanning helps you locate where the answers are found in the reading. Look for words and phrases similar to those found in the questions as you scan the text.

To maintain your reading speed, it is better not to pause to look up vocabulary words if you can guess their meaning from the context. Look up only those words that you need to know to understand the main ideas of the text. If you have determined that you will need to understand a text in detail, you can reread the important passages and look up more key words or all words that you do not know.

These reading strategies will enable you to grasp the writer's purpose and point of view without reading every word of a text. If you first define your purpose for reading, you will make better use of the strategies. For example, if you are reading to prepare for an objective quiz, you will need to read and study in more detail than if you are preparing for a discussion of main ideas. Reading strategies will improve the speed with which you are able to complete an assignment or research task, as well as your comprehension. Reading strategies are an essential first step for exploring the surface of a text so that you can locate that which you need to read in more detail.

III. Vocabulary building strategies

1. It is useful to buy a notebook or to keep a file on your laptop that you will use only for vocabulary.
2. When you learn one word, learn 2-4 related words from the dictionary.
    For example, if you look up 'judge', you will also find 'judgment', 'judicial', 'judiciary'.
3. Write the context (one sentence) in which you heard or read the word. If you are not sure of an appropriate context, ask a native speaker how s/he would use that word in a sentence. Without the context, sometimes memorizing a definition is not very useful.

4. Keep a list of prefixes and suffixes that you know and that you are learning. Those most commonly used come from Latin, and knowing them can help you guess the meaning of a word that you do not recognize, otherwise.
5. Practice using the word that you have just noted in conversation or in writing to help you remember the meaning.
6. When you record a word in your notebook, note also if it may or must be followed by a preposition, or a gerund or infinitive. Learn the words together as a unit.
    Example: Learn 'to rely on someone/something', not just 'to rely'.
7. Find out if a verb is transitive or intransitive, and include that in your notebook entry. Dictionaries will include this information with 'v.i.' or 'v.t.' or sometimes 'I' or 'T' after the word. It is important to know this because a verb that is transitive and never intransitive must have a direct object. An intransitive verb never has an object. Therefore, only transitive verbs may be used in the passive voice.
    Example: Learn 'to forward something'. That way, you will remember that you cannot write a sentence with 'to forward" without a direct object.
    He will forward to you (incorrect sentence)
    He will forward the letter to you. (correct sentence)
    It will be forwarded to you. (correct sentence)
8. In your notebook, record idioms and phrasal verbs in their contexts as you encounter them in conversation or in writing.

IV. Paraphrasing

Paraphrasing is basic to writing a summary. The term paraphrasing is used almost synonymously with writing a summary to mean restating the main ideas of another writer in your own words. Paraphrasing is also used to mean rewriting a sentence in detail, while maintaining all the meaning of the original.

Whenever you refer in your writing to the work of other writers, you must give credit where credit is due. This is the most important purpose of citations. You do not want to deprive another writer of the acknowledgement and recognition that a citation represents. At the same time, you do not want to subject yourself to the possibility of being accused of plagiarism. Whether or not it was your intent to take credit for the work of another writer, being accused of plagiarism can damage your student record or career. More than self-protection, however, the motive for avoiding plagiarism should be respect for the work of other writers. In addition, citations will allow your readers to locate the work for which you have created an interest through your writing and to read it in more detail.

You will need to acknowledge in a footnote not only those writers whom you quote directly, but also those whose work you paraphrase. If you choose to include a direct quote, that is, the exact words of another writer, those words must be enclosed with quotation marks. As noted in the introduction to this textbook, the correct citation forms for the legal profession are described in the "Bluebook".3.

Paraphrasing a sentence involves preserving all the meaning of the sentence while altering the grammatical structure and/or vocabulary. Paraphrasing a sentence is often used to clarify the meaning of a sentence, after citing it. You may also choose to paraphrase a sentence that is central to the writer's purpose or to yours. Finally, lawyers must be able to paraphrase a statute.

Exercise II-1- paraphrasing a sentence:

Rewrite each of the following sentences in the following two ways. First, clarify the meaning by changing the underlined key term. Second, write a possible next sentence that clarifies the meaning of the original sentence.

Example:

I have found a lot of prospects in my job search.
a. I have found a lot of interesting possibilities in my job search.
b. Now I am waiting to hear from the employers to whom I have applied for a job.

1. That country is one of the most advanced nations in the world.
2. Specialization in your profession can give you an advantage in the job market.
3. The local government of that town is very corrupt.
4. My neighbors seem like very conventional people.
5. Medicine has made great progress in recent decades.
6. The resort offers a variety of recreational activities.
7. He thinks his roommate is antisocial.
8. We are living in troubled times.
9. The new student union is energy-efficient.
10. His parents were concerned about his morals.

The most usual form of paraphrasing occurs after one writer reads another writer's ideas, reflects on or discusses their meaning, and then later describes them in his or her own words, usually in a condensed form. In this sense, writers may paraphrase an entire article or highlight one or more paragraphs in their own words.

Exercise II-2-paraphrasing a paragraph:

In pairs, choose one of the following paragraphs, and write a paraphrase of the paragraph in one or two sentences.

```
1. " Because 'sustainable' modifies 'development', it is first important
to understand what development means. Although Americans understand
development to mean the transformation of a field or woodlot into
housing or a mall, development has a different meaning at the
```

international level. Since the end of World War II, the United States and most of the world community have successfully sought greater peace and security, economic development, and social development or human rights. They have also sought national governance that supports these goals, even though they recognize that international efforts are also needed. As understood internationally, these are the four elements of development. This understanding of development grew out of the experiences of the last world war and the great depression that preceded and contributed to it, and a firm desire to ensure that the conditions that led to them would not occur again. More positively, development is intended to foster human freedom, opportunity, and quality of life." 4.

2. "There is thus a considerable international law foundation for development, which is reflected as well by international laws. Moreover, it is increasingly evident that the economic, social, and security goals of development are interdependent. That is, failure to achieve each of these goals compromises a country's ability to achieve the others. Social and economic development are impossible in the absence of peace. Economic and social development are themselves interrelated. Countries that have emphasized education, health and related aspects of social development tend to have the best economic performance.5.

3. "For a great many people and governments, this model of development has been synonymous with progress. Development has also been a central feature of the aspirations of the international community since the end of World War II. The treaties on which this model was built, however, did not refer to the environment. Environmental degradation was seen, if at all, as the incidental or necessary price of progress."6.

Exercise II-3-interpreting a statute:

Reading statutes often requires paraphrasing that includes all the meaning of the first sentence in the reworded writing.

In pairs, read the principles from the Rio Declaration on Environment and Development to which you have been assigned. Then write a paraphrase for each.

RIO DECLARATION ON ENVIRONMENT AND DEVELOPMENT

U.N. Doc. A/CONF.151/26;31I.L.M.874 (1992)
Signed: June 13, 1992

Preamble

The United Nations Conference on Environment and Development

Having met at Rio de Janeiro from 3 to 14 June 1992,

Reaffirming the Declaration of the United Nations Conference on the Human Environment, adopted at Stockholm on 16 June 1972, and seeking to build upon it,

With the goal of establishing a new and equitable global partnership through the creation of new levels of cooperation among States, key sectors of societies and people,

Working towards international agreements which respect the interests of all, protect the integrity of the global environmental and developmental system,

Recognizing the integral and interdependent nature of the Earth, our home,

Proclaims that:

Principle 1

Human beings are at the centre of concerns for sustainable development. They are entitled to a healthy and productive life in harmony with nature.

Principle 2

States have, in accordance with the Charter of the United Nations and the principles of international law, the sovereign right to exploit their own resources pursuant to their own environmental and developmental policies, and the responsibility to ensure that activities within their jurisdiction or control do not cause damage to the environment of other States or of areas beyond the limits of national jurisdiction.

Principle 3

The right to development must be fulfilled so as to equitably meet developmental and environmental needs of present and future generations.

Principle 4

In order to achieve sustainable development, environmental protection shall constitute an integral part of the development process and cannot be considered in isolation from it.

Principle 5

All States and all people shall cooperate in the essential task of eradicating poverty as an indispensable requirement for sustainable development, in order to decrease the disparities in standards of living and better meet the needs of the majority of people of the world.

Principle 6

The special situation and needs of developing countries, particularly the least developed and those most environmentally vulnerable, shall be given special priority. International actions in the field of environment and development should also address the interests and needs of all countries.

Principle 7

States shall cooperate in a spirit of global partnership to conserve, protect and restore the health and integrity of the Earth's ecosystem. In view of the different contributions to global environmental degradation, States have common but differentiated responsibilities. The developed countries acknowledge the responsibility that they bear in the international pursuit of sustainable development in view of the pressures their societies place on the global environment and of the technologies and financial resources they command.

Principle 8

To achieve sustainable development and a higher quality of life for all people, States should reduce and eliminate unsustainable patterns of production and consumption and promote appropriate demographic policies.

Principle 9

States should cooperate to strengthen endogenous capacity-building for sustainable development by improving scientific understanding through exchanges of scientific and technological knowledge, and by enhancing the development, adaptation, diffusion and transfer of technologies, including new and innovative technologies.

Principle 10

Environmental issues are best handled with the participation of all concerned citizens, at the relevant level. At the national level, each individual shall have appropriate access to information concerning the environment that is held by public authorities, including information on hazardous materials and activities in their communities, and the opportunity to participate in decision-making processes. States shall facilitate and encourage public awareness and participation by making information widely available. Effective access to judicial and administrative proceedings, including redress and remedy, shall be provided.

Principle 11

States shall enact effective environmental legislation. Environmental standards, management objectives and priorities should reflect the environmental and developmental context to which they apply. Standards applied by some countries may be inappropriate and of unwarranted economic and social cost to other countries, in particular developing countries.

Principle 12

States should cooperate to promote a supportive and open international economic system that would lead to economic growth and sustainable development in all countries, to better address the problems of environmental degradation. Trade policy measures for environmental purposes should not constitute a means of arbitrary or unjustifiable discrimination or a disguised restriction on international trade. Unilateral actions to deal with environmental challenges outside the jurisdiction of the importing country should be avoided. Environmental measures addressing trans-boundary or global environmental problems should, as far as possible, be based on an international consensus.

Principle 13

States shall develop national law regarding liability and compensation for the victims of pollution and other environmental damage. States shall also cooperate in an expeditious and more determined manner to develop further international law regarding liability and compensation for adverse effects of environmental damage caused by activities within their jurisdiction or control to areas beyond their jurisdiction.

Principle 14

States should effectively cooperate to discourage or prevent the relocation and transfer to other States of any activities and substances that cause severe environmental degradation or are found to be harmful to human health.

Principle 15

In order to protect the environment, the precautionary approach shall be widely applied by States according to their capabilities. Where there are threats of serious or irreversible damage, lack of full scientific certainty shall not be used as a reason for postponing cost-effective measures to prevent environmental degradation.

Principle 16

National authorities should endeavour to promote the internalization of environmental costs and the use of economic instruments, taking into account the approach that the polluter should, in principle, bear the cost of pollution, with due regard to the public interest and without distorting international trade and investment.

Principle 17

Environmental impact assessment, as a national instrument, shall be undertaken for proposed activities that are likely to have a significant adverse impact on the environment and are subject to a decision of a competent national authority.

Principle 18

States shall immediately notify other States of any natural disasters or other emergencies that are likely to produce sudden harmful effects on the environment of those States. Every effort shall be made by the international community to help States so afflicted.

Principle 19

States shall provide prior and timely notification and relevant information to potentially affected States on activities that may have a significant adverse trans-boundary environmental effect and shall consult with those States at an early stage and in good faith.

Principle 20

Women have a vital role in environmental management and development. Their full participation is therefore essential to achieve sustainable development.

Principle 21

The creativity, ideals and courage of the youth of the world shall be mobilized to forge a global partnership in order to achieve sustainable development and ensure a better future for all.

Principle 22

Indigenous people and their communities, and other local communities, have a vital role in environmental management and development because of their knowledge and traditional practices. States should recognize and duly support their identity, culture and interests and enable their effective participation in the achievement of sustainable development.

Principle 23

The environment and natural resources of people under oppression, domination and occupation shall be protected.

Principle 24

Warfare is inherently destructive of sustainable development. States shall therefore respect international law providing protection for the environment in times of armed conflict and cooperate in its further development, as necessary.

Principle 25

Peace, development and environmental protection are interdependent and indivisible.

Principle 26

States shall resolve all their environmental disputes peacefully and by appropriate means in accordance with the Charter of the United Nations.

```
                    Principle 27
     States and people shall cooperate in good faith and in a spirit
of partnership in the fulfillment of the principles embodied in this
Declaration and in the further development of international law in the
field of sustainable development.
```

Exercise II-4-summarizing a statute:

On the internet, look up the Health Insurance Portability and Accountability Act of 1996 (HIPAA), Public Law 104-191. In one paragraph, write a summary of the purpose of the Act and several of its requirements. If there are any implications of this act for either health care professionals or consumers on which you would like to comment, add your analysis in one or two sentences or in an additional paragraph.

V. Structures with "but for"

In U.S. tort law, the "but for" test is used to determine causation in negligence cases. Using "but for" is interchangeable in sentence structure and meaning with using "were it not for". For example:

```
But for his fiancee's support, he would not have succeeded.
Were it not for her support, he would not have succeeded.
```

Both of these examples may also be stated with an if-sentence:

```
If his fiancée had not supported him, he would not have
succeeded.
```

Exercise II-5-writing "but for" sentences:

The following situations represent potential tort and/or contract litigation within the context of corporate law.

In pairs, paraphrase the information about the following situations to which you have been assigned by writing a "but for" sentence that describes the alleged negligence of one party. Then write an if-sentence with the same meaning.

1. Company A is using Company B's trademark. Company B has lost money this year.

> **Example:** Company B would not have lost money but for Company A's use of its trademark.

2. The employee, using the company car to go to lunch at a restaurant, backed into the fence surrounding the restaurant, causing extensive damage to the fence.

3. There was ice on the steps of the office building. The employee fell on the ice and sprained his ankle.

4. The seller delivered the goods one week late. The buyer's company lost many customers.

5. The shareholders failed to invest enough money to cover the prospective liabilities of the company. As a result, the company went bankrupt.

6. A client was robbed in the lobby of the building belonging to the corporation. There was no security guard on duty.

7. A director did not attend any board meetings. The shareholders wanted to prove that his absences caused a loss to the company.

8. A tree on the company's property next to the public parking lot fell onto a customer's car. The roof of the car was damaged.

VI. Writing a Summary

If your purpose is to summarize in essay form a book or article by another writer, your essay will be devoted to that objective, and therefore, like other essays, will include an introduction and a conclusion. Each main idea that you highlight could be described in more detail in a body paragraph. The conclusion will restate the purpose and summarize the essay, but will not introduce any information. However, you may add an opinion or recommendation for future study.

Exercise II-6:

1. Read the following description of the history of the U.S. corporation. Identify three main ideas.

```
                Historical Sketch of the Corporation

    "The modern corporation did not rise up in one blazing moment of
inspiration. Instead, we can trace its current attributes to various
earlier times and forms. The idea of an amalgamation of persons forming
a separate juridical personality moved from Greece, to Rome, to the
continent, and to England. Originally, perpetual separate existence in
England was reserved for ecclesiastical, municipal, and charitable
bodies whose existence was conferred by sovereign grant. The idea of
common ownership by a body of passive investors originates from joint
stock-trading companies, such as the East India Company (a monopoly
franchise) in the early 1600's. A combination of continuity of life,
```

centralized management, financial interests in profits, transferability of shares, and limited liability for private business existed in the 1700's in the form of complex deeds of settlement-an unincorporated association!

"These concepts came to the American colonies. At first, private corporations, like political municipalities, had to receive a special charter from the state legislature. Legislatures granted charters on a case-by-case basis to non-commercial associations (such as churches, universities, and charities) that wanted the convenience of perpetual existence and to commercial associations (such as banks, navigation companies, canals, and turnpikes) with special public purposes and large capital needs. As the needs for capital (and thus incorporation) increased during the early 1800's, states began to enact general incorporation statutes for specified, usually capital-intensive, businesses. From the beginning, many feared the concentrated economic power inherent in the corporation device. Eventually, the U.S. corporation evolved in the mid-1800's into a legal form available to all, though subject to significant statutory restrictions.

"During the late 1800's, two major trends, leading in opposite directions, shaped modern U.S. corporate law. The first trend led to restraints on business activities. In the 1880's, Congress created the Interstate Commerce Commission to regulate the railroad monopolies; in 1890 and 1916, Congress passed anti-trust legislation (the Sherman and Clayton Acts) to combat consolidations of corporate economic power; in the early 1900's, states enacted 'blue sky' laws to deal with fraud in the sale of corporate securities; and in the 1930's, Congress passed a series of securities laws aimed at abusive management practices in interstate securities markets.

"The other trend led to a liberalization of state corporation statutes. In the late 1800's, to attract incorporation revenues, some states amended their statutes to lift limits on the amount of capital that a corporation could raise, to permit corporate ownership of other corporations, and generally, to increase the flexibility available to corporate management. Eventually, Delaware won this race, which some have called a scurrilous 'race to the bottom' and others an efficiency-producing 'race to the top'. Today, most large, publicly-traded U.S. corporations are incorporated in Delaware."7.

VII. Writing an Abstract

An abstract usually contains approximately 100 words, in one paragraph. Writers of journal articles may submit abstracts when they search for an appropriate publisher for their manuscript or when they respond to a call for papers for a conference. Abstracts often appear at the beginning of a published article in a journal. The importance of preparing abstracts underscores the importance of writing summaries.

Exercise II-7

As if you were the writer, in one paragraph, write an abstract for the "Historical Sketch of the Corporation" from the exercise for "Writing a Summary" above.

VIII. Writing a Case Brief

Briefing a case means writing a summary of it. Depending on a case's complexity, your purpose for reading it, and the nature of a course or class requirements, you may choose to write a brief in various ways. The outline of a brief generally includes:

1. the title of the case and its citation
2. the parties
3. the procedural history
4. the facts of the case
5. the issue, usually presented in question format
6. the arguments of each party
7. the holding and the rule that was formed by the holding
8. the court's reasoning

A brief may also include your comments or reaction to the case, which you might use in future writing or participation in a class discussion.

Exercise II-8:

Find the website for the U.S. Supreme Court. Look up the syllabus of <u>Ashcroft, Attorney General v. American Civil Liberties Union et al.</u>, No. 03-218. Argued March 2, 2004-Decided June 29, 2004. (A case syllabus does not contain any portion of the opinion of the Court.) Discuss the following in pairs or as a group:

a. What is the First Amendment? What does it have to do with this case?

b. What is COPA? Did the Court find that COPA is unconstitutional? Why or why not?

c. What is your analysis of this case? What are some of the possible implications for parents, children, and society of this decision?

Exercise II-9:

Write a brief of the case based on the syllabus.

Exercise II-10 (optional):

Look up the entire text of the case. Read the opinion of the Court. Do you agree or disagree with all or part of the Court's reasoning?

CHAPTER TWO-Grammar Review

Essential and Non-Essential Relative Clauses

1. The relative pronouns "that" and "which" are interchangeable when they refer to non-living things <u>and</u> are found in an essential clause.
2. "That" may be used to refer to people (and other living things) in an essential clause.
3. "Which" may be used in either an essential or a non-essential clause, but is not used to refer to people.
4. "Who" is generally used only for people, although some writers use "who" to refer to other living things, as well as all pets.
5. "Whom" is the objective form of "who" (direct object, object of a preposition) and is required in formal writing. (While the correct use of "whom" is never incorrect in speaking, its usage is becoming less frequent.)

Essential and non-essential clauses/punctuation

The purpose of a relative clause is to identify and describe the noun to which it refers. Commas are similar to parentheses with relative clauses and thus, indicate information that is descriptive, but not needed to identify the noun that the clause follows. Because essential clauses mean those that are necessary to identify the noun they follow, they are not set off with commas. Clauses beginning with "which", "who", and "whom" may be considered either essential or non-essential in meaning to the sentence. Clauses beginning with "that" indicate an essential clause.

```
1. The man whom you saw in the library teaches corporate law.
2. Professor Smith, whom you saw in the library, teaches
   corporate law.
3. In the library, you saw Professor Smith, who teaches corporate
   law.
4. In the library, you saw a man who teaches corporate law.
5. There are two professors with the last name "Smith". In the
   library, you saw Professor Smith who teaches corporate law.
```

As a general rule, when a name of a person or place is provided, the clause that follows is considered non-essential. Although the clause may contain important descriptive information, it is not essential to identify the person or place you are talking about.

```
6. The child who is in the garden is my son.
```

> 7. (The elementary school today gave an award for perfect attendance to a child.) The child, who is in the garden, is my son.

Sometimes, whether a clause is essential or not depends on the context. In example #7, we assume that the child has been identified in preceding sentences, so the fact that he is now in the garden is non-essential to knowing which child the writer means.

In example #6, there has been no preceding identification, so "who is in the garden" answers the question "Which child?" and is, therefore, essential.

> 8. The woman who was here yesterday is one of our oldest friends.
> 9. The woman that was here yesterday is one of our oldest friends.
> 10. (We just received an email from a woman.) The woman, who was here yesterday, is one of our oldest friends.

Example # 10 is similar to #7. The clause is non-essential because of preceding identifying information. Examples #8 and 9 are synonymous. However, "that" could not be used in example #10, as it may only be used in essential clauses, and therefore, does not follow a comma.

Exercise II-11:

In pairs, add commas where necessary. Decide which pronouns may be substituted with "that", if any. Assume there is no preceding identifying information, unless it is provided.

```
1. Betty and John who recently got married were not in class today.
2. My friends who recently got married were absent today.
3. The professor who is visiting our campus gave an interesting lecture.
4. Professor Caldwell who is visiting our campus gave an interesting lecture.
5. The vegetables which we had in the restaurant were delicious.
6. Vegetables which we should eat every day are not expensive at the market.
7. The Kyoto Protocol which was not ratified by the U.S. has been incorporated in part into New Jersey state law.
8. A treaty which is not ratified is not binding.
```

In which of the following sentences do all students want to become trial lawyers? What does the other sentence mean?

```
9. The law students who want to become trial lawyers are required to take Moot Court.

10. The law students, who want to become trial lawyers, are required to take Moot Court.
```

CHAPTER FOUR

WRITING A REPORT & WRITING A REACTION

I. Writing a Report

Reports represent a summary of factual information. A report, sometimes called a survey in a law journal, may give an overview of events within a given period, for example, but does not include an analysis of the information. An analysis would be needed, however, to write a reaction to the reported information or to write a comparison or a persuasive article.

Exercise III-1:

In pairs or small groups, find information on one of the following topics, and prepare a report for the class.

a. Why are so many companies incorporated in the state of Delaware?
b. What is the Model Business Corporation Act? How many states use it as the basis for their corporation statutes?
c. What is the purpose of the Sarbanes-Oxley Act of 2002? Describe the main points of this legislation.
d. Briefly describe the following business organizations: sole proprietorship, general partnership, limited partnership, limited liability company, corporation.
e. Briefly describe the following six essential elements of an enforceable contract: mutual assent, consideration, legal competency, lawful object, time limit, legal format. Are all oral contracts that have these elements enforceable?

II. Writing a Reaction

In general, a reaction is an essay that includes not only a summary of some or all of another writer's ideas, but also the first writer's own opinion. However, instead of appearing in the conclusion of a summary, your opinion in a reaction becomes the central theme of the essay. Your opinion and the summary are woven together throughout your discussion. The first sentence of a reaction and often the title will reflect your opinion. Expressing your opinion is the purpose of writing the reaction.

Letters to the editor of a newspaper are examples of reactions. Theater, movie, restaurant, and book reviews by professional critics are also reactions. Lawyers and law students often write reviews of books or incorporate ideas from books or journal articles to support our arguments in a research paper or article.

Moreover, the primary purpose for writing an article might be to react to an issue, event, or legal development. As a lawyer, you may need to write a reaction to recent cases as they may affect a case at hand and to include this content in an office memo whose purpose is to predict a legal outcome. You may also choose to include a reaction in a business letter. Finally, law students in a seminar may be called on to write reactions to all or part of a reading assignment and sometimes to share those reactions via email with the professor and other seminar students in preparation for a class discussion.

A reaction essay may or may not be written with the primary intent to persuade the reader. In addition to being a form of persuasive writing, a reaction may also overlap with the rhetorical mode of comparisons. If you want to react to the viewpoint of another writer, for example, you might compare that viewpoint with those of one or more other writers.

Sometimes the most difficult part of writing a reaction is writing clear objective statements that are supported with relevant examples and statistical data, where applicable. Writing a reaction often represents an exercise of free speech. However, an effective reaction must be clearly understood by the audience with well-documented examples that are not based purely on an emotional response. If you are reacting to a social problem or current event, you will strengthen your essay by including your recommendation for possible alternatives, solutions, or at least, next steps.

Essay Example B- (A Reaction)

Reaction to "The Advantages of Living in a Small Town"

The essay, "The Advantages of Living in a Small Town" (Essay Example A) presents several important reasons why people might choose to live in a small town. The most striking example involves community life.

The writer indicates that relationships are formed in neighborhoods and then often reinforced in other contexts such as schools or businesses. The smaller population of a town means that the likelihood of meeting the same people on a regular basis is greater than in a city. In a city, more often each context involves a completely separate group of people. Moreover, in a city, it is not always customary to establish a relationship with neighbors solely because they live near us.

The strength of relationships that develop in small towns seems advantageous not only socially, but also emotionally. According to Abraham Maslow's famous hierarchy of needs 8., everyone has a need to feel a sense of belonging, as well as safety. Knowing we live surrounded by people who will come to our assistance in a time of difficulty undoubtedly helps us sleep better at night. Knowing we may be needed, in turn, by the same people adds to our sense of belonging.

Neighbors in a small town, therefore, can add to the support that an extended family may give. Small town residents share a bond that can help individuals and families grow and thrive, as well as endure times of crisis. While the term "community" is used in many contexts, many people have never known the small town experience of true community life.

Exercise III-2:

In pairs or as a group, analyze the writing of the above reaction. To which point or points from Essay A does the writer react? How does the writer expand on that theme?

III. Reading

U.S. Supreme Court and Equal Protection

The U.S. Supreme Court (the Court) reviews cases in which a state or local government has allegedly violated a Bill of Rights provision, such as freedom of religion or freedom of speech. All provisions of the Bill of Rights apply to the states because the Court determined that the Bill of Rights has been incorporated into the Due Process clause of the Fourteenth Amendment.

The Court applies three levels of scrutiny to analyze the constitutionality of such state and local laws.

1. Rational Basis test- A law is upheld if it is rationally related to a legitimate government purpose. (Here the challenger has the burden of proof, and the government usually wins.)
2. Intermediate Scrutiny- A law is upheld if it is substantially related to an important government function. (The government has the burden of proof.)
3. Strict Scrutiny- A law is upheld if it is necessary to achieve a compelling government purpose. (The government has the burden of proof.)

Strict scrutiny is applied to any state or local law that appears to discriminate according to race. Intermediate scrutiny is always applied to laws that appear to discriminate according to gender. Rational basis has been applied to laws that appear to discriminate against people according to age.

In addition, strict scrutiny is applied to government discrimination against ethnic origin and against non-citizens. This is usually interpreted to mean non-citizens who have permanent visas (green cards). However, only a rational basis test is used when the government requires citizenship for employment and other activities that concern self-government, such as voting, serving on a jury, or being a public school teacher, probation officer, or police officer.

Strict scrutiny is applied to laws that appear to interfere with the right of citizens to travel within the U.S. (but not abroad) and with their right to vote. So far, only a rational basis test has been applied to discrimination based on disability, age, and wealth (discrimination against poor people).

The U.S. Supreme Court is the "highest law of the land", and therefore, states must apply the Court's holdings as a minimal standard of regulation. In other words, in equal protection cases, states must apply at least a rational basis test to discrimination based on disability, age, and wealth, and at least intermediate scrutiny to discrimination based on gender. States may, however, require intermediate or strict scrutiny for such discrimination if they so choose.

Exercise III-2:

1. Read and discuss the above information.

2. Choose a theme for a reaction essay based on the reading, and write a title reflecting that theme. (For example, how do you feel about the Court's decision to apply intermediate, rather than strict, scrutiny to gender discrimination, while applying strict scrutiny to racial discrimination? What might have been the Court's reasoning?)

3. Write a thesis sentence for the introduction of your proposed reaction essay, and then write the topic sentences for three body paragraphs and the conclusion.

Exercise III-3:

1. Read Regents of the University of California v. Bakke 18 Cal.3d 34, 553 P.2d 1152.

2. Discuss this case in view of the above information regarding equal protection. Identify one or more themes that interest you about the case and discussion.

3. Write a reaction based on your chosen theme and/or

4. Write a reaction based on your outline for Exercise III-2-3 above.

IV. Reading- Legal Theory

Positivism

"Scientific methodology informs legal thought not only in shaping our sense of what laws are, but in supporting positivism as a school of legal philosophy. Curiously, the relationship between legal and scientific positivism has received little attention, even though the similarity of the two is patent and illuminating. Scientific positivists accept hypotheses as true in the popular sense only if they meet agreed upon criteria of validation used in mustering, confirming, and disconfirming evidence. The principle of nonfalsifiability holds that a proposition is scientifically meaningful only if we can imagine evidence that would constitute its refutation. The important point about positivist methodology is that claims must be validated by a method open to all. Empirical evidence meets that requirement of universal accessibility, while the authority of tradition or a holy book does not. Science based on the Bible or on Aristotle is binding only on those who accept these works as authorities.

"Legal positivism shares the same commitment to an agreed upon method of validation. Like the scientific positivist, the legal positivist cannot bear the thought of a proposition that is neither verifiable nor falsifiable, but that, as it were, just floats in the body of law waiting to be believed or disbelieved. Alleged rules of law require anchors. They must be tied down to a legislative organ that enacts, repeals and modifies laws. That legislative organ must, in turn, be able to trace its authority to a constitution, which in turn must find its grounding either, in Hans Kelsen's version, in a "basic norm" of the system or, in H.L.A. Hart's idiom, in a "rule of recognition" that legitimates the constitution and thus the entire legal system. After all, why do we assume that fifty-five men meeting in Philadelphia could write a constitution that would continue to bind the United States for generations and centuries after they and those in the state ratifying conventions were dead? Underlying every constitution is the simple fact that the people accept it; and they show this continuing acceptance in their daily behavior of living, more or less, by the rules of the legal system.

"The critical assumption for legal positivists is that law cannot be treated simply as a phenomenon that exists, as nature and the universe exist. In law as well as in science, positivism requires an agreed-upon method for deciding whether a particular proposition is valid under the system, namely, whether it is a law. Legal positivists insist upon a method for verifying and falsifying hypotheses about the contents of the legal system. For any particular proposition of law, they want to be able to determine whether it is valid or invalid, according to the internal rules of the system. It is valid if it can be traced to an authoritative source, which is itself validated by the basic norm of the system; it is invalid if it is simply asserted without having an anchor in an authoritative source.

"For purposes of further discussion, the simplest working definition of positivism is this: Positivism holds that all law is enacted law. " 9.

Exercise III-4:

Read the above passage about the concept of legal positivism. In one paragraph, write a summary of the reading.

Exercise III-5:

1. Read the U.S. Supreme Court case, Roper v. Simmons.
2. Identify the arguments raised on both sides. Is there any argument that is particularly persuasive to you?

Exercise III-6:

Develop your summary about legal positivism (Exercise III-3) into a reaction essay by responding to the following questions:

1. Did the U.S. Supreme Court's decision in <u>Roper v. Simmons</u>, in your opinion, reflect positivism or natural law?

2. Do you think it is an appropriate role for the Court to base some or all of its decisions on morality? Do you think that the Court did so in this case?

CHAPTER THREE-Grammar Review

Subject-verb inversion

At the beginning of a sentence, after some words and phrases with a negative meaning, the subject and verb are inverted.

Examples:

```
a.  Only if you practice will you succeed in developing new
skills.
   You will not succeed in developing new skills unless you
practice.
   If you do not practice, you will not succeed in developing new
skills.

b. If you practice, not only will you succeed, you will also
develop confidence.
   If you practice, you will succeed and also develop confidence.

c. He did not know how to cook when they got married, nor did he
know how to iron his clothes.
   Neither did he know how to iron his clothes.
   He did not know how to iron his clothes, either.

d. No longer will the teacher remind the students to arrive on
time, but instead, he will mark them absent when they are late.
   The teacher will not remind the students to arrive on time any
longer.
```

N.B.: **1.** Subject-verb inversion following a negative is also used in informal conversation.

> **Example:** Student A-I don't like to stay up late.
> Student B-Neither do I.

2. Although "neither" and "either" generally indicate two beings or items, they may also be used in a list of more than two.

> **Examples:**   a. Either Jane or John will meet you at the
> airport.

b. Neither my husband nor I can attend the meeting.

c. Neither rain, nor snow, nor heat, nor gloom of night stays these couriers from the swift completion of their appointed rounds." This statement is attributed to the Greek historian, Herodotus (484-425 B.C.) and is still used to describe the ideals of modern mail delivery.

3. However, "none" is used instead of "neither" to replace the nouns when there are more than two items.

Example: a. She and her husband have a previous engagement. Neither of them is going to the **meeting**.

b. There are five students in the study group, but none of them can attend this **evening**.

Exercise III-7:

The landmark case, Marbury v. Madison 5 U.S. 137 (1803) helped define the role of the U.S. Supreme Court in evaluating the constitutionality of laws. In his decision, John Marshall stated, "It is emphatically the province and duty of the judicial department to say what the law is. Those who apply the rule to particular cases must of necessity expound and interpret that rule. If two laws conflict with each other, the courts must decide on the operation of each."10.

In pairs, briefly discuss your reaction to this quotation and to the role of the judiciary that it describes. Then write sentences that relate to the quotation or to your discussion and that begin with each of the following:

only if, not only, neither, no longer, unless, not unless, until, not until.

CHAPTER FOUR

WRITING A COMPARISON

Comparing and contrasting usually are inexorably intertwined to the extent that the term "comparison" may inherently include both likenesses and differences. Comparisons may be used for definitions and descriptions. They are also an important means of making complex topics more understandable. Comparisons can strengthen your arguments in persuasive writing by showing how one course of action is preferable to another.

A comparison written within a broader essay may help readers draw fine, but important, distinctions between two highly similar legal cases, for example. On the other hand, a comparison may convince readers that two seemingly disparate cultures or legal systems have much in common.

I. Outlining a comparison

Two structures of comparisons serve as bases for comparative writing. In the first, the writer determines three or more points to compare between two items and then develops an outline that emphasizes the two items.

A. Comparing items

```
Introduction

Living in a small town

    a. Convenience for doing errands
    b. Community life
    c. Proximity to recreational activities/nature

Living in a large city

    a. Convenience for doing errands
    b. Community life
    c. Proximity to recreational activities/nature

Conclusion

    Discussion of the similarities and differences
reviewed in the two body paragraphs.
```

The writer using this structure devotes one paragraph to small towns and one paragraph to large cities, (one paragraph for each of the two items being compared), while discussing all three points in each. The actual comparing and contrasting are found in the conclusion.

In the second form of comparative writing, each of the points to be compared is highlighted in a separate paragraph. A comparison of the similarities and differences about each point is found within the body paragraphs.

B. Comparing points

Introduction

Convenience of doing errands

    a. Small town
    b. Large city

Community life

    a. Small town
    b. Large city

Proximity to recreational areas and nature

    a. Small town
    b. Large city

Conclusion

While the first outline may be more suitable for highlighting similarities, the second is useful for a more detailed presentation of contrasts. The first may also be used when the writer's main purpose is to describe, rather than to persuade. In that case, it is not necessary to choose precisely the same points to discuss for each item, nor is it necessary to prove that one item is preferable to the other.

Due to the nature of the process of comparing, a comparative essay relies on connectors more than does any other rhetorical mode. For example, connectors list the similarities or differences (first, next, in addition, finally). They introduce contrast (on the other hand, whereas, in contrast), as well as the result of differences (consequently, therefore). They show that some differences have little consequence (although, even though, while). While transitions lend coherence to paragraphs and to all forms of essays, the use of connectors is particularly important to connecting the ideas in a comparison.

Essay Example C-Comparison/comparing items

The following comparison is intended to be descriptive, not persuasive. Therefore, the two items being compared serve as the paragraph topics, while the points described about each are not precisely parallel, and the writer is not concerned about persuading the reader that one item is more advantageous than the other. The title of the comparison also reflects the descriptive purpose.

Essay C

Life in a City or Life in a Small Town: Life is Good

Many people prefer living in a large city. Convenient public transportation, cultural and social activities, and employment opportunities attract many residents. At the same time, other people would rather live in a small town, finding greater convenience there, as well as closer community life, and more recreational activities.

In a large city, it is possible to travel conveniently by various means of public transportation. Many urban dwellers prefer not to own a car and can then avoid the stress of driving in traffic and looking for parking places. They benefit from the health advantages of walking to the train or bus stop or to their final destinations.

People who prefer to live in large cities often cite the variety of social and cultural activities that are available and that allow them to meet friends with similar interests. They frequently attend concerts and the theater or visit museums. They also enjoy finding international fairs and restaurants that bring the whole world into close proximity.

Many city dwellers first choose to live in a large city because of the greater number of employment opportunities. They can also find highly specialized jobs, as well as a variety of settings in which to work, and a greater likelihood of jobs with flexible working hours.

In a small town, on the other hand, it is important and even necessary to own a car. However, car ownership is much more convenient than in a city. There are always available parking spaces, and often the commercial area is centralized, allowing residents to complete several errands, including food shopping, without moving their cars. While the commercial areas may be farther from their house than in a city, small town residents do not usually have to contend with traffic jams.

People who live in small towns enjoy a close-knit community life that is unknown in large cities. Small town residents tend to meet their neighbors and to make themselves available to assist their neighbors when needed. Living in a small town may contribute to a sense of well-being through the sense of safety and belonging that community life inspires. Friendships in small towns are continually reinforced, as neighbors may meet each other in a variety of situations, including through their children's schools and at work.

Small town dwellers have access to recreational opportunities that also include plenty of parking. While city dwellers spend countless minutes and even hours waiting on long lines, the need to wait on line for a movie, for example, is practically non-existent in a small town. Moreover, outdoor recreational activities are usually accessible within minutes of a small town. Residents of small towns may enjoy hiking and bicycling while feeling close to nature.

In summary, there are many differences between life in a large city and life in a small town. Each one has its own characteristics and distinct advantages. Where you choose to live will depend on your individual priorities.

Exercise IV-1:

Writing an outline for a comparison

1. As a class, choose three points to compare about legal systems.

2. In pairs (of students from different countries),

a. discuss how the legal systems of each of your countries compare regarding the three items.

b. If you are working individually, note how the legal system of your country and that of another country with which you are familiar compare regarding the three items.

c. Choose one of the above structures for writing a comparison, depending on your purpose for writing. Write an outline for a five-paragraph comparative essay.

II. Reading

Asakura v. City of Seattle
265 U.S. 332, 44 S.Ct. 515, 68 L.Ed. 1041 (1924).

Mr. Justice Butler delivered the opinion of the court.

Plaintiff in error is a subject of the Emperor of Japan, and since 1904, has resided in Seattle, Washington. Since July, 1915, he has been engaged in business there as a pawnbroker. The city passed an ordinance, which took effect July 2, 1921, regulating the business of pawnbroker and repealing former ordinances on the same subject. It makes it unlawful for any person to engage in the business unless he shall have a license, and the ordinance provides "that no such license shall be granted unless the applicant be a citizen of the United States." Violations of the ordinance are punishable by fine or imprisonment or both. Plaintiff in error brought this suit in the Superior Court of King County, Washington, against the city, its Comptroller and its Chief of Police to restrain them from enforcing the ordinance against him. He attacked the ordinance on the ground that it violates the treaty between the United States and the Empire of Japan, proclaimed April 5, 1911, 37 Stat.1504; violates the constitution of the state of Washington, and also the due process and equal protection clauses of the Fourteenth Amendment of the United States. He declared his willingness to comply with any valid ordinance related to the business of pawnbroker. It was shown that he had about $5000 invested in his business, which would be broken up and destroyed by the enforcement of the ordinance. The Superior Court granted the relief prayed. On appeal, the Supreme Court of the State held the ordinance valid and reversed the decree. The case is here on writ of error under Section 237 of the Judicial Code.

Does the ordinance violate the treaty? Plaintiff in error invokes and relies upon the following provisions: "The citizens or subjects of each of the High Contracting Parties shall have liberty to enter, travel, and reside in the territories of the other to carry on trade, wholesale and retail, to own or lease and occupy houses, manufactories, warehouses and shops, to employ agents of their choice, to lease land for residential and commercial purposes, and generally to do anything incident to or necessary for trade upon the same terms as native citizens or subjects, submitting themselves to the laws and regulations there established…The citizens or subjects of each…shall receive, in the territories of the other, the most constant protection and security for their persons and property…"

A treaty made under the authority of the United States "shall be the supreme law of the land; and the judges in every State shall be bound thereby, any thing in the constitution or laws of any State to the contrary notwithstanding." Constitution, Art. VI, Section 2.

The treaty-making power of the United States is not limited by any express provision of the Constitution, and, though it does not extend "so far as to authorize what the Constitution forbids," it does extend to all proper subjects of negotiation between our government and other nations. The treaty was made to strengthen friendly relations between the two nations. As to the things covered by it, the provision quoted establishes the rule of equality between Japanese subjects while in this country and native citizens. Treaties for the protection of citizens of one country residing in the territory of another are numerous, and make for good understanding between nations. The treaty is binding within the State of Washington. The rule of equality established by it cannot be rendered nugatory in any part of the United States by municipal ordinances or state laws. It stands on the same footing of supremacy as do the provisions of the Constitution and laws of the United States. It operates of itself without the aid of any legislation, state or national; and it will be applied and given authoritative effect by the courts.

The purpose of the ordinance complained of is to regulate, not to prohibit, the business of pawnbroker. But it makes it impossible for aliens to carry on the business. It need not be considered whether the State, if it sees fit, may forbid and destroy the business generally. Such a law would apply equally to aliens and citizens, and no question of conflict with the treaty would arise. The grievance here alleged is that plaintiff in error, in violation of the treaty, is denied equal opportunity.

By definition contained in the ordinance, pawnbrokers are regarded as carrying on a "business". A feature of it is the lending of money upon the pledge or pawn of personal property which, in case of default, may be sold to pay the debt. While the amounts of the loans made in that business are relatively small and the character of property pledged as security is different, the transactions are similar to loans made by banks on collateral security…We have found no state legislation abolishing or forbidding the business. Most, if not all, of the States provide for licensing pawnbrokers and authorize regulation by municipalities. While regulation has been found necessary in the public interest, the business is not on that account to be excluded from the trade and commerce referred to in the treaty. Many worthy occupations and lines of legitimate business are regulated by state and federal laws for the protection of the public against fraudulent and dishonest practices. There is nothing in the character of the business of pawnbroker which requires it to be excluded from the field covered by the above quoted provision, and it must be held that such business is "trade" within the meaning of the treaty. The ordinance violates the treaty. The question in the present case relates solely to Japanese subjects who have been admitted to this country. We do not pass upon the right of admission or the construction of the treaty in this respect, as that question is not before us and would require consideration of other matters with which it is not now necessary to deal. We need not consider other grounds upon which the ordinance is attacked.

Decree reversed.

Sei Fujii v. California
38 Cal.2d 718, 242 P.2d 617(1952).

Gibson, Chief Justice.

Plaintiff, an alien Japanese who is ineligible to citizenship under our naturalization laws, appeals from a judgment declaring that certain land purchased by him in 1948 had escheated to the state. There is no treaty between this country and Japan which confers upon plaintiff the right to own land, and the sole question presented on this appeal is the validity of the California alien land law.

UNITED NATIONS CHARTER

It is first contended that the land law has been invalidated and superseded by the provisions of the United Nations Charter pledging the member nations to promote the observance of human rights and fundamental freedoms without distinction as to race. Plaintiff relies on statements in the preamble and in articles 1, 55 and 56 of the Charter.

It is not disputed that the charter is a treaty, and our federal Constitution provides that treaties made under the authority of the United States are part of the supreme law of the land and that the judges in every state are bound thereby. U.S. Const., art. VI. A treaty, however, does not automatically supersede local laws which are inconsistent with it unless the treaty provisions are self-executing. In the words of Chief Justice Marshall: A treaty is "to be regarded in courts of justice as equivalent to an act of the Legislature, whenever it operates of itself, without the aid of any legislative provision. But when the terms of the stipulation import a contract-when either of the parties engages to perform a particular act, the treaty addresses itself to the political, not the judicial department; and the Legislature must execute the contract, before it can become a rule for the court." Foster v. Neilson, 1829, 2 Pet.(U.S.) 253,314,7 L.Ed.415.

In determining whether a treaty is self-executing courts look to the intent of the signatory parties as manifested by the language of the instrument, and, if the instrument is uncertain, recourse may be had to the circumstances surrounding its execution.

In order for a treaty provision to be operative without the aid of implementing legislation and to have the force and effect of a statute, it must appear that the framers of the treaty intended to prescribe a rule that, standing alone, would be enforceable in the courts.

It is clear that the provisions of the preamble and of Article 1 of the charter which are claimed to be in conflict with the alien land law are not self-executing. They state general purposes and objectives of the United Nations Organization and do not purport to impose legal obligations on the individual member nations or to create rights in private persons. It is equally clear that none of the other provisions relied on by plaintiff is self-executing. Article 55 declares that the United Nations "shall promote…universal respect for, and observance of, human rights and fundamental freedoms for all without distinction as to race, sex, language, or religion," and in Article 56, the member nations "pledge themselves to take joint and separate action in cooperation with the Organization for the achievement of the purposes set forth in Article 55." Although the member nations have obligated themselves to cooperate with the international organization in promoting respect for, and observance of, human rights, it is plain that it was contemplated that future legislative action by the several nations would be required to accomplish the declared objectives, and there is nothing to indicate that these provisions were intended to become rules of law for the courts of this county upon the ratification of the charter.

The language used in articles 55 and 56 is not the type customarily employed in treaties which have been held to be self-executing and to create rights and duties in individuals. For example, the treaty involved in Clark v. Allen, 331 U.S. 503, 507-508, 67 S.Ct. 1431, 1434, 91 L.Ed.1633, relating to the rights of a national of one country to inherit real property located in another country, specifically provided that such national shall be allowed a term of three years in which to sell the (property)...and to withdraw the proceeds..." free from any discriminatory taxation. In Nielsen v. Johnson, 279 U.S. 47, 50, 49 S.Ct. 223, 73 L.Ed.607, the provision treated as being self-executing was equally definite. There each of the signatory parties agreed that "no higher or other duties, charges, or taxes of any kind, shall be levied" by one country on removal of property therefrom by citizens of the other country "than are or shall be payable in each state, upon the same, when removed by a citizen or subject of such state respectively." In other instances treaty provisions were enforced without implementing legislation where they prescribed in detail the rules governing rights and obligations of individuals or specifically provided that citizens of one nation shall have the same rights while in the other country as are enjoyed by that country's own citizens. *Asakura v. Seattle,* 265 U.S. 332,340,44 S.Ct.515,516,68 L.Ed.1041;

It is significant to note that when the framers of the charter intended to make certain provisions effective without the aid of implementing legislation, they employed language which is clear and definite and manifests that intention. For example, Article 104 provides: "The Organization shall enjoy in the territory of each of its Members such legal capacity as may be necessary for the exercise of its functions and the fulfillment of its purposes." Article 105 provides: "1. The Organization shall enjoy in the territory of each of its Members such privileges and immunities as are necessary for the independent exercise of their functions in connection with the Organization." In Curran v. City of New York, 191 Misc. 229, 77 N.Y.S.2d 206, 212, these articles were treated as being self-executory.

The provisions in the Charter pledging cooperation in promoting observance of fundamental freedoms lack the mandatory quality and definiteness which would indicate an intent to create justiciable rights in private persons immediately upon ratification. Instead, they are framed as a promise of future action by the member nations. Secretary of State Stettinius, Chairman of the United States delegation at the San Francisco Conference where the charter was drafted, stated in his report to President Truman that Article 56 "pledges the various countries to cooperate with the organization by joint and separate action in the achievement of the economic and social objectives of the organization without infringing upon their right to order their national affairs according to their own best ability, in their own way, and in accordance with their own political and economic institutions and processes."

The humane and enlightened objectives of the United Nations charter are, of course, entitled to respectful consideration by the courts and legislatures of every member nation, since that document expresses the universal desire of thinking men for peace and for equality of rights and opportunities. The charter represents a moral commitment of foremost importance, and we must not permit the spirit of our pledge to be compromised or disparaged in either our domestic or foreign affairs. We are satisfied, however, that the charter provisions relied on by plaintiff were not intended to supersede existing domestic legislation, and we cannot hold that they operate to invalidate the alien land law.

> (Although the California Alien Land Law originally prevented Asians from owning land, in 1952 it affected Japanese aliens primarily, because at that time, they were still barred from becoming U.S. citizens.)
>
> **N.B.** (The court concluded that the California Alien Land Law of 1920 was invalid because it violated the Fourteenth Amendment of the U.S. Constitution.)

Exercise IV-2:

Read the above international law cases.

Note the issue, the procedural history, the facts, and the holding of each case, as well as the court's reasoning. These points provide key areas for writing a comparison.

N.B.- The U.S. Constitution regards an international treaty as the law of the land, "trumping", or taking priority over, state law, but only when the Court finds that the treaty is "self-executing" because it is already incorporated into U.S. law or because Congress develops implementing legislation in response to the treaty.

Exercise IV-3:

Write a comparison of the Asakura v. City of Seattle and the Sei Fujii v. California cases, noting similarities and differences. Be sure to discuss the meaning of "self-executing" treaties, as well as "implementing law". Also discuss whether the U.N. Charter has or should have the same authority as a treaty.

III. Reading

Jurisdiction in U.S. Law

To remand-to send a case back to a lower court. For example, when a judge in an Appeals Court holds that more fact-finding needs to be done, s/he can remand the case to the trial court.
To remove-to send a case from a state to a federal court.

Criminal procedure-

A state has jurisdiction, i.e. jurisdiction to prosecute, if either the crime or the result happened in that jurisdiction. Whether the defendant is a citizen of that state does not matter.

Civil procedure-

A. Personal jurisdiction (In which state will the plaintiff sue the defendant?) Personal jurisdiction (over an individual or entity) may be established by domicile, presence in the state when served with process, or consent. More difficult cases arise when there is lesser contact with the jurisdiction, particularly in determining jurisdiction over corporations. The famous Supreme Court case known as International Shoe v. Washington 326 U.S. 310 (1945) represented a shift from "consent" or "presence" as the model for jurisdiction, which had been described in an equally famous case, Pennoyer v. Neff 95 U.S. 714 (1877), to one of "minimum contacts such that jurisdiction is consistent with traditional notions of fair play and substantial justice".

Minimum contacts must result from "purposeful availment", i.e. defendant's voluntary act. The possibility of being sued in that state must also have been foreseeable (not the lawsuit itself, but the possibility of jurisdiction). If the contact with the forum is very minimal, relatedness between the contact and the claim will be considered. The defendant may complain that the distance from where s/he lives to the forum is inconvenient. This is not allowable as an excuse, unless the forum puts the defendant at a severe disadvantage in the litigation, which is very hard to show. The state's interest in providing a forum for its citizens will also be considered.

B. Subject matter jurisdiction (In which court, federal or state?) After determining personal jurisdiction, it is necessary to determine subject matter jurisdiction. Federal courts can hear only certain types of suits, primarily diversity of citizenship and federal question.

1. Diversity of citizenship- This means that the action must be between citizens of different states, or between a citizen of a state and a foreign resident. There is no diversity of citizenship jurisdiction if any plaintiff is a citizen of the same state as any defendant. For individuals, citizenship is the state of one's domicile, which is established by one's presence in a state with the intent to make it one's home.

For corporations, domicile is not used. Instead, citizenship equals :

a. all states in the U.S. where incorporated (usually only one) and

b. the state where the corporation has its principle place of business. Corporations, unlike individuals, can have more than one state citizenship at a time. However, a corporation has only one principle place of business. This usually means either the headquarters or the state where the corporation does most production or service activity.

For partnerships and other unincorporated associations, the citizenship of all members is used. Therefore, it would be impossible to have diversity of citizenship jurisdiction with a partnership whose members represent all fifty states.

The second requirement for diversity of citizenship is that the amount in controversy must be more than $75,000.

2. Federal question cases- The complaint must show a right or interest that is founded substantially on federal law or the constitution. Citizenship is irrelevant, and there is no requirement for the amount in controversy. Plaintiff is suing to enforce a federal right. Some federal question cases have exclusive federal jurisdiction. These include patent infringement, as well as federal antitrust and securities claims.

3. Venue- (In which federal district?) In any federal case, whether diversity or federal question, the plaintiff may lay venue in any district where all defendants reside or where a substantial part of the claim arose.

If there is no district in the U.S. that corresponds to these options, which occurs when all defendants do not reside in the same district and the claim arose overseas, then venue can be laid, in federal question cases, in any district where the plaintiff is found, or in diversity cases, in any district where any defendant is subject to personal jurisdiction.

a. forum non conveniens (FNC)- If there is a far more convenient and appropriate court elsewhere, a court (judge) may dismiss the case to let the plaintiff sue the defendant there. That other court is usually in a country other than the U.S., so removal would be impossible. The decision is based on public factors (what law applies, whether the fact finder needs to visit the site of the events) and private factors (where witnesses and evidence are). The fact that the plaintiff may recover less in that court does not make dismissal improper. FNC dismissal is almost never granted if plaintiff is a resident of the present forum.

Exercise IV-4:

Read and discuss the above information. Then write a timed essay (30 minutes) on one of the following topics:

1. Write a comparison between jurisdiction in the U.S. and that in another legal system. In your essay, identify three points to compare.

2. Write a reaction to the information about U.S. jurisdiction.

Exercise IV-5:

In pairs, develop a hypothetical case. Include details that are relevant to determining jurisdiction. Share your example with the class, and ask them to determine in which court of which state your hypothetical case may be heard. If your hypothetical could be both a criminal and a torts case, ask the class to decide how that could make a difference to the jurisdiction.

```
Example: Plaintiff's domicile is the state of New York. He was
driving on an interstate highway in Massachusetts when the
traffic suddenly slowed because of a snowstorm. A truck owned by
the Major Trucking Company with headquarters in Georgia was
behind his car. The truck driver, who is a resident of New
Hampshire, did not reduce his speed accordingly and collided with
plaintiff's car, causing injuries to plaintiff, as well as damage
to plaintiff's vehicle.
```

CHAPTER FOUR-Grammar Review

Parallel structure

1. When a sentence contains a list of words, phrases, or clauses, the items in the sequence should have the same grammatical structure.

> **Example (incorrect):**
> ```
> We like skiing, skating, and to go for a bike ride.
> ```

"To go for a bike ride" has an infinitive, whereas the other items are gerunds. Therefore, the sentence does not have parallel structure. The sentence may be edited in either of the following ways:

> **Examples (correct):**
> ```
> We like to go skiing, skating and bicycling.
> We like skiing, skating, and bicycling.
> ```

2. Each phrase or clause in sequence in the same sentence must have parallel structure.

Examples (incorrect):
1. He had breakfast, met an old friend by chance, and then the plane left before he got to the airport.
2. Do you think it's rude to talk on the phone and keep watching t.v.?

Examples (correct):
1. He had breakfast, met an old friend by chance, and then missed the plane.
2. Do you think it's rude to talk on the phone and to watch t.v. at the same time?

3. The grammatical structure of a sentence may appear parallel, but the meaning may require clarification.

Example (incorrect):
Paying a penalty for not recycling and making plastic bags illegal are important ways to protect the environment.

In the above sentence, although gerunds are used to introduce both phrases, the agents implied by the gerunds differ. The sentence still needs to be edited.

Examples (correct):
Imposing a penalty for not recycling and making plastic bags illegal are important ways to protect the environment.

Being required to pay a penalty for not recycling and (being) prohibited from using plastic bags are important ways to protect the environment.

4. To achieve parallel structure in a comparative sentence, the actual items being compared must be compared grammatically. This is usually done through the use of pronouns.

Examples (incorrect):
The places we visited on this vacation were more unusual to us than last year.(The writer is not comparing a vacation to a year, so this structure is incorrect.)
The books in the public library are more diverse than the University.(The writer is not comparing books to a University, so this structure is also incorrect.)

Examples (correct) :
The places we visited on this vacation were more unusual to us than those we visited last year.
The books in the public library are more diverse than those in the University.

ExerciseIV-5:

Edit the following sentences so that they have parallel structure:

1. Sustainable development relates to preserving natural resources and to human rights.

2. Do you believe that developed countries have an obligation to control pollution as well as in developing countries?

3. By choosing to drive smaller vehicles, we can help reduce air pollution, our dependency on oil, and it will save us money.

4. They are not only committed to walking to work to help the environment, but also it is good exercise.

5. Clearing a forest in the old days was considered the same as to make progress.

6. Either the government makes recycling mandatory or people have to pay for garbage disposal.

Subject-verb agreement

1. Following most expressions of quantity, whether the verb is singular or plural is determined by the noun that follows.

Examples:
a. Some of the cases that we discussed represent the most recent decisions in internet copyright law.
b. Some of the information is relevant to my research.
c. Three quarters of the students are from this state.
d. One quarter of their income is spent on their mortgage.
e. A lot of law schools were represented at the Moot Court competition.
f. A lot of tax money is spent every year to repair highways.

Exceptions (all of the following take singular verbs):

One of, each of, every one, either, neither, none of, everyone, someone

N.B. : In informal English, "neither" and "none of" are often used with plural verbs.

Examples of exceptions:
a. One of the cases is on point.
b. Each of my courses will have a final exam.
c. Every one of the LLM students is required to write a thesis.
d. Either my employer or my professor is going to the conference.
e. Neither environmental law nor international law is tested on the Bar exam.
f. None of the assignments is easy.

2. In sentences with "there + be", whether the verb is singular or plural is determined by the noun that follows.

Examples:
```
a. There is a difference between the dissenting opinions.
b. There are several differences among the dissenting opinions.
```

N.B. The preposition "between" is used distinguish two items, while "among" is used for more than two.

3. The expression "a number of" is always followed by a plural noun and a plural verb.

Examples:
```
a. A number of decisions support that premise.
b. A number of students are transferring to another school.
```

4. Expressions of quantity with "of" may be used in adjective clauses. Only "whom", "which", and "whose + noun" can be used as the objects of a preposition, such as "of".

Examples:
```
a. We read several articles, some of which we will incorporate
into our group research project.
b. The law firm will hire five interns for the summer, all of
whom must have completed one year of law school.
```

5. The noun "people" is always plural.

Example:
```
Many people are planning to attend the lecture.
```

CHAPTER FIVE

WRITING TO PERSUADE

Writing to persuade (argumentation) represents a rhetorical mode that is inherent to the nature and purpose of many functions of a lawyer's professional role. As we have seen, the ability to write a summary, a reaction, and a comparison enhance the power to persuade. However, writing a persuasive essay, brief, or other document includes additional key elements.

Guidelines

Here are some guidelines for writing to persuade:

1. Write a clear *thesis statement* that shows either your position or the question that you will answer. This is usually included in the first paragraph of the essay. The title of the essay may also reflect your opinion. On the other hand, the title may be stated as a question that you will answer in your essay through presenting both sides of the question and then showing the reader that you have chosen the better argument.

For example, if the title of your essay is, "`Living in a Small Town Proves More Advantageous than Living in a Large City`", you have presented your opinion and also equated your opinion with fact. You would identify three points of comparison and focus on each in a separate paragraph.

Your title might also be, "`Which is More Advantageous, Living in a City or in a Small Town?`" In the second example, you would answer the question in your essay after reviewing several advantages of both alternatives.

While stating opinion as fact is a device that may be employed in any rhetorical mode, it is especially important in persuasion. In academic writing, the first person normally is not used, even when the writer is expressing an opinion, because it appears informal. At the same time, omitting the first person may result in statements of opinion that sound like fact. Compare the potential difference in persuasive impact of the following sentences:

```
My reaction is that the new legislation will be ineffective in
implementing the international treaty.

The new legislation will be ineffective in implementing the
international treaty.
```

2. Consider your *audience*. How much and what kind of information will be necessary to persuade them?
If your audience of readers is comprised of large city dwellers, for example, you may need to present more convincing details about life in a small town. If the readers plan to move to the U.S., but have never visited the U.S. before, you might offer more description of life in a large U.S. city.

3. Consider your *topic*. Decide whether for your topic it would be more effective to present and refute opposing arguments, or rather to focus only on arguments that support your point of view.

This consideration relates to the previous one regarding audience. If you think that most people prefer large city living to small town living, you will also need to include opposing arguments to show that large cities have many disadvantages that small towns do not have. Also, if you include only the advantages of small towns, your essay may lack persuasiveness if readers feel that there are obvious disadvantages to small towns. In that case, your essay needs to present those disadvantages and then refute them, i.e. tell why they are exaggerated, or how other factors offset them, etc.

4. Use *logic*. Emotional appeals in writing to persuade are usually considered ineffective.

Objective descriptions will add to the persuasive power of your writing.

5. Use *precision*. Avoid indefinite words, or phrases that sound indefinite, such as 'may', 'might', 'it seems'.

```
Close-knit communities enjoy the lower crime rate of life in a
small town.
```

The above is a more persuasive statement than the following.

```
Close-knit communities may be a factor that contributes to the
low crime rate of life in a small town.
```

6. Use *factual statements* to present your opinion. In developing your supportive arguments, use accurate information and statistics.

7. To refute an opposing opinion or argument, first write a brief *summary* or *paraphrase* of that point of view for the reader.

For example, you can summarize one of the advantages of living in a large city before proceeding to show either that this is not really an advantage or that the comparable point with regard to a small town is preferable.

```
a. (summarize an opposing argument) Living in a large city is
often equated with having a thriving and varied social life, with
the opportunity to meet countless people who share similar
interests.
```

```
b. (refute the opposing argument)However, small towns also offer
a social life that includes not only sharing a variety of
recreational activities, but also building long-lasting
friendships because people in small towns tend to move less
frequently than large city dwellers.
```

8. Write a *restatement* of your arguments in the conclusion.

In all academic writing, there should be a concluding paragraph that restates the thesis and briefly summarizes the discussion. Whether you present a thesis or a question, you can highlight the relevant arguments in the conclusion that led to your position.

Essay Examples A and D (Persuasion);
Essay Example C (Comparison)

Essay Example A in Chapter One and reprinted below, in addition to being an example of basic essay structure, could also be used as an example of a persuasive essay that uses the approach of presenting only one side of an argument, i.e., the advantages of living in a small town. However, it is generally more persuasive to raise at least some of the opposing arguments, as well, and then to refute them.

Essay A

The Advantages of Living in a Small Town

    Many people prefer living in a large city. Urban employment opportunities, cultural and social activities, and convenient public transportation attract many residents. City dwellers may disparage life in a small town, especially one that is remote from all urban areas.
    There are, however, many advantages to living in a small town. The first advantage to living in a small town is the convenience of daily errands. Small towns generally provide shopping areas within minutes by car of each residential area. These areas offer ample parking spaces, allowing residents to complete a variety of errands, including buying gas, taking clothes to the dry cleaner, and shopping for food without going to separate locations or spending time searching for parking.
    Another advantage is the close-knit community of small town life. Neighbors in small towns usually introduce themselves and maintain frequent contact. In addition, they are likely to meet in other social, school, or business situations, strengthening their ties. Close-knit communities tend to offer emotional support in times of stress and crisis. Small town residents do not move frequently, so these supportive friendships may continue for many years.
    Finally, the proximity to recreational areas and natural beauty is an important advantage to living in a small town. Just as doing errands is not so time-consuming, going to the movies or to a sports event is convenient and does not usually involve waiting in long lines nor searching for parking spaces. Residents of small towns also have places to enjoy nature, while hiking or bicycling, for example, within minutes of their homes.
    In conclusion, many city dwellers overlook the advantages of living in a small town. Living in a small town often means experiencing more convenience for doing daily errands, a close-knit community where people assist each other in times of crisis, and proximity to recreational areas and natural beauty. While many people prefer living in a large city and even disparage small town life, residents of small towns continue to enjoy many features that city dwellers overlook.

Essay Example C, in Chapter Four and reprinted below, provides an example of a comparison that is intended to describe, not to persuade, and compares items, rather than points. In Essay Example D, which follows, the writer intended to show that one alternative, living in a small town, is better than the other, living in a city. The title reflects the writer's opinion, but is presented as fact. Each paragraph of the essay's body focuses on one point, and exactly the same point is discussed for each item. By using this format, the writer presents the same three advantages to living in a small town as presented in Essay A, but in Essay D, also shows that a large city does not have these three advantages.

Essay Example C (descriptive comparison)

Life in a City or Life in a Small Town: Life is Good

Many people prefer living in a large city. Convenient public transportation, cultural and social activities, and employment opportunities attract many residents. At the same time, other people would much rather live in a small town, finding greater convenience there, as well as closer community life, and more recreational activities.

In a large city, it is possible to travel conveniently by various means of public transportation. Many urban dwellers prefer not to own a car and can then avoid the stress of driving in traffic and looking for parking places. They benefit from the health advantages of walking to the train or bus stop or to their final destinations.

People who prefer to live in large cities often cite the variety of social and cultural activities that are available and that allow them to meet friends with similar interests. They frequently attend concerts and the theater or visit museums. They also enjoy finding international fairs and restaurants that bring the whole world into close proximity.

Many city dwellers first choose to live in a large city because of the greater number of employment opportunities. They can also find highly specialized jobs, as well as a variety of settings in which to work, and a greater likelihood of jobs with flexible working hours.

In a small town, on the other hand, it is more advisable and even necessary to own a car. However, car ownership is much more convenient than in a city. There are always available parking spaces, and often the commercial area is centralized, allowing residents to complete several errands, including food shopping, without moving their cars. While the commercial areas may be farther from their home than in a city, small town residents do not usually have to contend with traffic jams.

People who live in small towns enjoy a close-knit community life that is unknown in large cities. Small town residents tend to meet their neighbors and to make themselves available to assist their neighbors when needed. Living in a small town may contribute to a sense of well-being through the sense of safety and belonging that community life inspires. Friendships in small towns are continually reinforced, as neighbors may meet each other in a variety of situations, including through their children's schools and at work.

Small town dwellers have access to recreational opportunities that also include plenty of parking. While city dwellers spend countless minutes and even hours waiting on long lines, the need to wait on line for a movie, for example, is practically non-existent in a small town. Moreover, outdoor recreational activities are usually accessible within minutes of a small town. Residents of small towns may enjoy hiking and bicycling while feeling close to nature.

In summary, there are many differences between life in a large city and life in a small town. Each one has its own characteristics and distinct advantages. Where you choose to live will depend on your individual priorities.

Essay Example D (persuasion)

Choose Life in a Small Town and Enjoy Peace of Mind

Many people prefer living in a large city. City dwellers may disparage life in a small town, especially in one that is remote from all urban areas. There are, however, many advantages to living in a small town that do not exist in cities. Some of them are priceless, including peace of mind.

First, the convenience of daily life in a small town saves time and reduces stress. Small towns generally provide shopping areas that are located within minutes by car of each residential area. These areas include ample parking spaces, allowing residents to complete a variety of errands, including buying gas, taking clothes to the dry cleaner, and shopping for groceries without going to separate locations or spending time searching for parking.

While it is true that many people in large cities choose not to own a car because of the convenience of public transportation, the amount of groceries they can buy at one time is limited to what they can carry onto the bus or train. Moreover, the dry cleaner, post office, and gift shops are often found in different areas, not necessarily within walking distance of the supermarket. The inability to complete errands in a timely manner adds to the stress of life in a large city and diminishes the amount of available leisure time.

Second, small town dwellers enjoy a close-knit community life that cannot be found in a large city. Neighbors in a small town make an effort to meet each other, and these relationships are continually reinforced in other contexts, as neighbors are likely to meet again through their children's schools, at work, or at social activities. There is a sense of community that contributes to everyone's sense of belonging and safety, which according to Abraham Maslow's well-known hierarchy of needs 11., is vital to human well-being. Knowing we live surrounded by people who will come to our assistance in a time of difficulty undoubtedly helps us sleep better at night. Knowing we may be needed, in turn, by the same people adds to our sense of belonging.

However, while living in a city is often equated with having a thriving and varied social life with the opportunity to meet countless people who share similar interests, often social relationships in a city are scattered and somewhat superficial. People who meet at work do not always meet again in other contexts, for example. At the same time, city dwellers tend to move more frequently than small town residents, and relationships may not be as lasting. Finally, city dwellers do not always meet their neighbors, and the experience of an emotionally supportive community is generally unknown in the city.

Finally, the proximity to recreational areas and natural beauty is an important advantage to living in a small town. Just as doing errands is not so time-consuming, going to the movies or to a sports event is convenient and does not usually involve waiting in long lines or searching for parking. Residents of small towns also have places where they can enjoy nature, while hiking or bicycling, for example, within minutes of their homes. These activities tend to reduce stress. Although many cities have beautiful parks where hiking and bicycling are possible, as well as a sense of being closer to nature, for city dwellers, even recreation can be stressful because of traffic jams or crowded buses and long distances or waiting periods.

In conclusion, there are countless important advantages to living in a small town. The convenience of doing errands, making errands less stressful and time-consuming, the shared emotional support and lasting friendships of a close-knit community, the convenience of recreational facilities, and the proximity of areas of natural beauty all contribute to the priceless asset of peace of mind that is the primary advantage of living in a small town.

Exercise V-1:

1. Do you think that Essay D is more persuasive than Essay A? Explain.

2. Essay Example D (above) avoids arguments that could demonstrate the advantages of life in a city, such as museums, theater, international exhibitions, and employment options. These advantages of living in a large city were presented in Essay Example C, a comparison that was not intended to persuade. However, the writer purposely omitted them from the above persuasive essay. Do you think Essay Example D would be more persuasive if the writer had acknowledged additional advantages of living in a large city and then refuted them? Discuss.

3. In pairs, write an outline for a persuasive essay about the advantages of living in a large city. Include the examples from Essay C, as well as your own ideas.

Exercise V-2:

Choose one of the following four topics for writing to persuade:

1. The Berne Convention for the Protection of Literary and Artistic Works is an international treaty to which the U.S. is a signatory. The treaty was considered non-self-executing in the U.S., and therefore, implementing legislation was needed for the treaty to become U.S. law.
Article 6bis refers to the "moral right" of creators of works of art (authors).This right , recognized in other legal systems, primarily the French, is a non-transferable right that remains with the author and enables him or her to protect the integrity of the work legally against alteration, mutilation, and destruction, even after the copyright has been transferred. 12.
In the U.S., the owner of a copyright has the power to maintain or not the integrity of a work. However, this power usually does not

belong to the author, but rather to the publisher or producer of the art work, or even to an individual buyer of a sculpture or painting.

Section 106A, also known as the Visual Artists Rights Act (VARA), of the U.S. Copyright Act is the implementing legislation for Article 6bis. 13.

1.
   a. Read Article 6bis of the <u>Berne Convention for the Protection of Literary and Artistic Works.</u>
   b. Read Section 106A (VARA) of the <u>U.S. Copyright Act.</u>

   Discuss these readings in pairs or as a group. Choose your position individually. Write a persuasive essay entitled, "Does VARA put the U.S. in compliance with Article 6bis?"

2. Read <u>The Soering Case</u> European Court of Human Rights, Judgment of 7 July 1989, Series A, Vol. 161, 1989 WL 650110 (or another case that particularly interests you in U.S. or international law regarding capital punishment). Write a persuasive essay entitled, "Was (this case) decided correctly?"

3. According to the decision in the above case, the <u>Convention on Human Rights</u>, Article 3, states that "No one shall be subjected to torture or to inhuman or degrading treatment or punishment."
   In your opinion, does the so-called "death row phenomenon" constitute a violation of Article 3?

4. Choose an important legal or social issue facing your first country, the U.S., or the world. Write a persuasive essay describing both sides to this question and showing which side has the better argument.

CHAPTER FIVE--Grammar Review

Phrasal verbs

Phrasal verbs are two-word verbs whose meaning generally changes when combined with a preposition; the verb and preposition become one phrase. These are important to know for listening purposes because they are frequently used in U.S. English. However, it is equally important in academic writing to find a one word synonym for a phrasal verb, because phrasal verbs, like idioms, are generally considered too informal for academic writing.

Exercise V-3:

Edit the following sentences by finding a one-word synonym for each of the phrasal verbs:

1. This change in temperature has brought about many other changes around the world.
2. They wanted to keep up with all the cases in their field.
3. The boss asked her to stay late to look over the documents.
4. The professor pointed out that the house was now considered a historic landmark.
5. Luckily, he had saved his research paper onto a disk, because someone threw out his only hard copy.
6. The students decided to think over the assignment before choosing a topic.
7. The meeting was put off for a few days because of the snowstorm.
8. The student got a job in the library putting back all the books that are left on the desks.
9. The lawyer decided to look into the matter before accepting the case.
10. Because of the rumors, we decided to find out what had really happened.
11. The professor handed out copies of an article that he wanted the students to read.
12. They had to hand in their research papers on the last day of final exam week.
13. The meeting was called off because of the snowstorm.
14. We ran into an old friend in the cafeteria.
15. What will we do if the earth runs out of natural resources?

CHAPTER SIX

WRITING BUSINESS LETTERS

I. Overview

Writing a business letter may seem difficult because the phrases that native speakers might use may be unfamiliar. However, if you have achieved the proficiency of advanced level academic writing, you already have the most essential skills for writing business letters.

Here are some points to keep in mind:

1. Business letters in the U.S. are written in formal academic style. Even if the writer and recipient have a somewhat informal relationship in person, a business letter still reflects formality, primarily because it will serve as a written record and because the purpose of the letter is professional, not personal.

2. Business letters in the U. S. tend to reflect the cultural style of "getting to the point". The purpose of the letter is usually stated directly in the first sentence.

3. Business letters in the U.S., therefore, are generally as brief as possible.

II. Format/Titles

The block format is currently the most widely used for business letters. In this format, paragraphs are not indented. Both the sender's address and the recipient's formal name and address appear on the left side of the page, while the greeting, paragraphs, closing, salutation, and signature are all aligned at the same point on the left margin. (If the sender is using pre-printed letterhead or business stationery, that address might be in the center of the top of the page.) The recipient's name should be preceded by "The Hon." (meaning "the honorable", for a judge),"Dr." (for a medical doctor ,but for a Ph.D. usually used only if the business letter is related to his/her professional role), Mr.", or "Ms."

While some married and previously married women prefer the title "Mrs.", in a business letter, "Ms." is generally more acceptable if you are writing to a woman in her professional role. Identifying whether a professional woman is married or not is considered irrelevant, particularly since men do not reveal this information through their names and since both being married and not being married can be bases for professional discrimination against women .

If the recipient is a lawyer, usually the sender types "Attorney at Law" beneath the name. If the recipient is a judge, the name of the district usually appears under the judge's name and title.

III. Greetings

The most usual greeting in a business letter is "Dear" followed by the title (Judge,Mr.,Ms.,Dr.) and the last name of the recipient. If the sender is on a first-name basis with the recipient, the first name may be used. However, the recipient's name still will appear in formal form with the address above the greeting. The greeting "Dear" plus the name is always followed by a colon in a business letter.

IV. Beginning

The first sentence should state the purpose of the letter. Usually, this is the only sentence in that "paragraph".

Here are some opening sentences that are commonly found in business letters from lawyers:

```
1. The purpose of this letter is to (acknowledge receipt of …)

2. This is in reference to our phone conversation of July 1.
```

The latter sentence could be used to "follow up" on a phone call. It indicates that the main paragraph of the letter will contain information that the sender promised in the phone call. It might also be a reminder for the recipient to provide information as promised in the phone conversation.

```
3. This is to memorialize our phone conversation of July 1.
```

This sentence means that the letter will reiterate the substance of the phone conversation according to the sender and that the letter will serve as a record of the phone conversation. Such a letter will probably also state that the recipient should reply in writing if his/her recollection of the phone conversation differs.

```
4. This is to provide you with the results of my research about….
```

You will probably think of several ways to state this. Such statements may be used to inform a client about whether a lawyer thinks there is a viable case, or if there is, what the possible outcomes might be. You might also use this sentence when sending feedback to anyone about information you had promised to find.

```
5. This is to request a copy of…
```

Many business letters request documentation or more detailed information and serve as a record of the request.

```
6. This is to establish the scope of our firm's (my)
   representation regarding...
```

Some lawyers refer to such a letter as a "scope letter". It is very important to establish in writing with each client the basis and limits of your legal relationship with that client so that the client will not depend on you for assistance in other areas that you have not discussed. A scope letter can also protect you if a client sues you for negligence in other areas because of a false impression that you were his/her lawyer for every situation that might require a lawyer.

V. Middle

The middle of a business letter should, if possible, contain only one paragraph, and this paragraph should be related to the purpose as stated in the first sentence of the letter.

For example, in a "scope letter", the middle paragraph would describe the purpose and limits of the legal representation that you are providing.

VI. Pre-Closing

Usually, the pre-closing consists of 1-2 sentences, mainly for the purpose of courtesy. However, in the first sentence of a pre-closing, you may also include a reminder of what you need the sender to do or a restatement of what you will do.

Examples of the first sentence in a pre-closing:

```
1. If I can be of further assistance, please do not hesitate
   to call on me.

2. If you have any questions regarding this information,
   please do not hesitate to call my office.

3. As soon as I receive the above information from you, I will
   be in touch with you again as soon as possible.

4. Please call my office at your earliest convenience to
   schedule an appointment so that we can discuss this matter
   in more detail.

5. I will look forward to hearing from you at your earliest
   convenience.
```

Examples of the second sentence in a pre-closing:

```
1.   Thank you very much for contacting our firm.

2.   I will look forward to hearing from you at your earliest
convenience.

3.   Thank you very much for your attention (consideration)
(cooperation).
```

VII. Closing

The following closings are standard in U.S. business letters:

```
Sincerely,
Sincerely yours,
Very truly yours,
Yours truly,
Cordially yours,
```

N.B. Email:

In addition to the above, a broader range of less formal greetings and closings are found in business letters that are sent by electronic mail (email):

`Greeting-`

```
Hello ( first then last name, or first name only)
Hi, ( first name)
Dear All, (when addressing a group of more than two people)
```

`Closing-`

```
Regards,
My best regards,
Best,
Best wishes,
Kind regards,
```

VIII. Signature

A signature is important in a business letter because it gives the document authenticity.

Usually, the complete name of the sender is typed 3-4 spaces below the closing.

In the U.S., lawyers do not have a special title in direct address, that is, when others speak to them or write to them. Usually, they are called "Mr. Smith" or "Ms. Smith", or sometimes by their first name. However, the sender does not include "Mr." or "Ms." next to his/her name below the signature, although below the typed name, the sender might include "Attorney at Law".

Then the sender signs his/her name above the typed name. As in the greeting, a first name alone may be used if the sender and recipient have an informal relationship. However, even if a client calls you by your first name, it is preferable to sign business letters to clients with your complete name in case you need to use the letter as a legal record.

IX. Examples of Business Letters
I.
(Your business address if it does not appear on the letterhead)
July 1, 20__

Mrs. John Salada
333 Main Street
Small Town, N.Y. (zip code)

Dear Betty:

This is in reference to our phone conversation of July 1, 200_.

In order to determine whether our firm will represent you, we will need to review a copy of your employment contract.

I will look forward to receiving the contract from you at your earliest convenience.

Thank you very much for your consideration of our firm.

Sincerely,
Mary
Mary Lipton
Attorney at Law

II.
(your address)
July 1, 20__

Dr. Robert Twining
Main Street Group
3 Main Street
Small Town, N.Y. (zip code)

Dear Bob:

This is to memorialize our phone conversation of July 5, 200_ regarding the offer of part-time employment from City Hospital.

As I mentioned to you by phone, my supervisor and I have read the employment contract carefully and recommend that you not sign this part-time employment contract from City Hospital until you have clarified in writing whether City Hospital will permit you under this contract to continue working at Main Street Group as you had intended to do.

If I can be of further assistance, please do not hesitate to call on me.

Thank you very much for contacting our firm.

Sincerely,
William Folger (Bill)
William Folger
Attorney at Law

III.
(your business address)
July 1, 20__

Linda Maxwell, Ph.D.
School of Education
Local University
Local, N.Y. (zip code)

Dear Dr. Maxwell:

This is to establish the scope of our firm's legal representation regarding your employment contract.

As we discussed, our firm has agreed to read the employment contract that you have been offered by Large University, to meet with you to discuss its terms, and to advise you as to whether it is in your best interests to sign the contract.

This is the only agreement for legal representation that our firm has established with you.

Please call my office at your earliest convenience so that we can set up an appointment to discuss the contract in more detail.

I am looking forward to hearing from you at your earliest convenience.

Sincerely,
Jane Starbuck
Jane Starbuck

Exercise V-1:

Choose one of the following, and practice writing a business letter from a lawyer.

1. You are deciding whether to accept your client's case. Your client's boss insulted him. You need more information from the client regarding the details of what happened. Write a letter to your client asking for this information. Add your own details to the hypothetical. Include the following legal information for your client by paraphrasing it into non-legal language.

> Defamation is a tort for which money damages may be available.
> At least one other person must be present when the defaming statement is made.
> If the insult refers to professional competence, it is considered slander per se; that is, the victim will not need to prove damages.
> However, if the insult is actually part of a criticism of employee performance that may be comparable to an evaluation,

```
              it is possible that the employer's statement will not be
              found to be defamatory.
              Name-calling is usually not enough to constitute defamation.
```

2. Your client wants to change jobs. In an interview for a new job, she was told that she would have to sign an agreement that would prevent her from working in the northeast of the U.S. for a period of five years following her resignation. (This is sometimes called a "non-compete" agreement and may be valid, but it should be "reasonable".) There are also many other points in the contract with which she disagrees. Add your own details to the hypothetical. Your client would like you to negotiate a new contract for her. You ask her whether she signed a similar agreement with her current employer. You ask her to bring a copy of the agreement with her to a meeting in your office that has not yet been scheduled.

3. Your own hypothetical situation. Write a business letter that you will need to write in your current or future area of legal practice.

X. Reading –Corporate Law

Read the following passage, and answer the questions below within 30 minutes (or other appropriate time limit).

Corporations

```
     While there are many possible structuring devices for modern
businesses, the corporation is perhaps the most well known. A
corporation is a legal person through which businesses can enter into
contracts, own property, sue and be sued in court.14.

     A corporation's existence is distinct from that of its
shareholders and creditors, i.e. those who contribute capital, and from
its directors and officers, i.e. those who manage the business of the
corporation. The board of directors often delegates its power to
officers to take action that binds the corporation.15.

     The ownership interests of shareholders are freely transferable.
Directors and officers may resign at any time. Shareholders, as well as
directors and officers, are known as corporate insiders and are not
personally liable to outsiders for corporate torts or debts.16.

     Corporate law applies to the relationship between shareholders
and managers while relationships with outsiders are governed by
contract, tax, environmental, and labor laws.17. Each state of the U.S.
has its own corporation statutes that describe the rights of
shareholders, the powers of shareholders and management, and the
process for incorporating in that state.18.Judicial gap-filling, that
is, the role of the courts in making corporate law, usually pertains to
the fiduciary duties of the corporate board of directors.19.
```

State statutes generally codify standards of behavior for directors. These include the duty of care and the duty of loyalty. The duty of care means that directors will remain informed in their decision-making and management with the care with which other people in similar circumstances would perform. The duty of loyalty requires acting in the best interests of the corporation, and refraining from self-dealing by not usurping an opportunity of the corporation nor receiving an improper personal benefit.[20]

In the more than 150 years since the directors' duty of care has been recognized, few directors and officers have been held liable for mismanagement, not including cases involving illegality, fraud, or conflict of interest. This is because of the "business judgment rule"(bjr), which represents an attitude (a rebuttable presumption) more than an actual rule. The bjr assumes that directors do not breach their duty of care.[21]

The bjr is supported judicially because the bjr encourages those who are qualified to become directors, as well as to take risks on behalf of the corporation and its shareholders, thus possibly encouraging more investors to become shareholders. Courts also recognize that some lawsuits may be brought by those at odds with the corporation so that a breach of the duty of care may not be the real issue.[22]

Challengers of decisions made by directors bear the burden of overcoming the bjr by proving fraud, illegality, or conflict of interest, lack of a rational business purpose, or gross negligence.[23]

Exercise VI-2:

1. What is a primary advantage of forming a corporation?
2. What are the terms for the management and the investors of a corporation ?
3. What does corporate law mainly involve? What kinds of concerns do corporate law cases generally involve?
4. What are the duties of the directors of a corporation?
5. What is the business judgment rule?

CHAPTER SIX- Grammar Review

Verbs + gerunds or infinitives

A. A gerund is the –ing form of a verb that is used as a noun in a sentence.

B. Like verbs or adjectives with prepositions, verbs with gerunds or infinitives must be memorized. There is no rule for determining which preposition or structure follows. Whenever you learn a verb or adjective, learn the preposition or gerund/.infinitive structure that follows.

> For example, if you are learning the verb `to admit`, learn the phrase `to admit doing something.`

Please see Chapter Ten for a list of verbs that are followed by gerunds, verbs that are followed by infinitives, and verbs that may be followed by either.

C. In addition to following a verb, a gerund or an infinitive may function as the subject of a sentence.

```
Writing is hard work.
To write a book takes a long time.
```

D. Since gerunds are verb forms that can take the place of a noun in a sentence, they are preceded by a possessive, not objective, form of a noun or pronoun.

```
He was worried about my going out in the snow.(correct)
He was worried about me going out in the snow.(incorrect)

The guest speaker's being late inconvenienced everyone in the
audience.(correct)
```

Exercise VI-3:

In pairs, combine the following sentences by using a gerund phrase with a possessive:

```
1. The incumbent won the election. This shocked almost everyone.
2. Some of the students were always late. The professor asked to
meet with them after class.
3. The students in that law school tend to be very concerned
about human rights. You can find out more by reading their newsletter.
4. We did not have time to go to the party. Our friends who are
not in law school did not seem to understand the reason. (For review, what
is the difference between "our friends who are not in law school" and "our friends, who
are not in law school"?)
5. Marbury v. Madison is the case that clarified the role of the
Supreme Court in interpreting the U.S. Constitution. The employer asked
John in the interview whether he was familiar with the case.
6. Last summer, he worked as a student for the same firm in
another city. This was one of the reasons that the supervisor offered
him the job when he graduated.
```

Like/As

A. The primary difference between these two words is that "like" is a preposition and "as" is a conjunction. Keeping this distinction in mind will prevent many common errors with their usage.

Examples:
```
He works hard like his father.
He works hard as his father does.
```

N.B. In formal writing, "as" is followed by an inverted subject and verb:
```
He works hard, as does his father.
She was a lawyer, as were most of the participants in the
conference.
```

B. In addition to requiring different structures, "like" and "as" have different meanings in a comparison.

Examples:

```
She worked hard like a lawyer.
(She may not have been a lawyer, but she worked as hard as
lawyers work.)

She worked hard as a lawyer.
(When she was a lawyer, she worked hard.)
```

C. In informal spoken English, "like" is often used as a conjunction. However, this is incorrect in formal style.

Examples (incorrect):
```
He works hard like his father does.
```

D. The conjunction "as" is used in phrases that signify a mutual understanding.

Examples:
```
As we agreed, I am forwarding the signed contract.
As you know, construction will begin next week.
As you suggested in the meeting, we ought to document every
phone call that we make.
```

CHAPTER EIGHT

WRITING IN THE 'IRAC' FORMAT

I. Overview

The purpose of this section is to explain the "irac" format. Law students are not expected to know this format nor to be familiar with its use before beginning a J.D. or LLM program, and therefore, this section will serve merely as an introduction to "irac".

The "irac" format is particular to the U.S. "common law" or "case law" system in which the decisions of judges are used as precedents (rules) for future decisions of other judges in similar cases. In the U.S., judges use case law concurrently with statutory law in deciding a case.

The "irac" format represents an outline that lawyers use in writing legal documents. These include office memos, which are circulated within a firm. An office memo predicts the outcome of a case and, therefore, the likelihood that a client's problem indicates a valid legal claim and one that is reasonable for the firm to accept as a case. The "irac" format is also applied to appellate briefs, which are written to persuade a judge about the correct decision of a case on appeal.

II. Use of "irac" by law students

Law students who are required to write a hypothetical office memo or an appellate brief will use "irac" in the same manner that a practicing lawyer would use "irac" to write such documents. All law students in the U.S. use the "irac" format in answering essay questions on final exams for their classes that require examinations, as well as in writing Bar examination essays.

On a law school exam, sometimes the rules from hypothetical cases or statutes that the professor wants you to use in answering the exam question hypothetical are included. Sometimes you will need to form a rule from the hypothetical precedents. At the same time, you may be expected to apply a rule that is considered basic to legal knowledge, such as "but-for" in torts or the Miranda warnings in criminal law.24. You will have studied such rules in class as an inherent part of the course content, and your professor will likely have identified them as important to know for the exam. However, on both course exams and Bar exams, students are not normally expected to have memorized statutes or briefs of case precedents from which the rules originated. Moreover, the ability to apply the rule is generally considered the most important part of writing in the "irac" format and is usually given the most weight in grading.

III. IRAC

A. Introduction

"Irac" represents an outline for writing and an abbreviation for:

Issue
Rule statement (formed from relevant case precedents and statutes)
Application (of the rule to the case at hand)
Conclusion

Within a complex legal problem, there may be several sub-issues, each of which needs to be reviewed separately according to the "irac" model before an overall conclusion may be reached. In that case, the outline would include issue-rule-application, issue-rule-application, etc., till all issues have been presented, followed by the conclusion.

There may also be several rules that you will want to analyze that pertain to the same issue. The outline would then be issue-rule-application, rule-application, rule-application etc., followed by the conclusion.

B. Issue identification

Identifying or "spotting" the issues is an important skill for a lawyer and, therefore, is highly tested in law school and on the Bar exam. Lawyers must decide whether a prospective client has a valid claim within the problem that the client describes. The claim may contain more than one issue, or you may choose to reword the issue after reading the precedents, in order to distinguish your case from previous cases.

```
Example of a possible exam question:

    Imagine that your client is a businessperson who was robbed in
the lobby of a building owned by the ABC Corporation while your client
was waiting for the elevator to go to a meeting. Your client wants to
sue ABC Corporation for not employing a security guard, claiming that
ABC Corporation is responsible for the robbery. (Your client wants to
sue for the trauma of being a crime victim, which she can document
through subsequent medical or psychiatric appointments, as well as for
the cost of the items stolen.) Does your client have a valid claim?
```

The aspect of the case that your client presents is a tort case because your client wants to prove that she has been harmed through someone else's negligence for which she would like receive a monetary award (damages). There would also be a criminal case based on your client's report of the incident to the police. In the criminal case, the alleged robber would be the defendant and the state would be the prosecutor/plaintiff. Obviously, the alleged robber would hire a different lawyer. In the torts case, your client is the plaintiff, and the building owner is the defendant.

C. Issue statement

An issue may be expressed as a statement, but is often expressed as a direct question:

```
The issue is whether an owner of a building is liable for the
personal safety of people who enter the building.

Is the owner of a building liable for the personal safety of
people who enter the building?
```

Answering this question affirmatively requires showing that building owners have a duty of care in such situations.

D. Rule statement

In order to establish that there is a duty of care, research would first involve searching for relevant statutes. (On exams, these will normally be provided if students are expected to apply them.)

Assuming that no statute exists that requires building owners to hire a security guard, the next step would be to search for previous similar tort cases with the goal of finding at least one that was decided in favor of the victim.

U.S. Supreme Court cases, of course, are the most persuasive, followed by federal court decisions. Holdings within the same jurisdiction as that of the case at hand, particularly in higher courts of that jurisdiction, would also be persuasive.

Briefly state the holdings of these cases and formulate a rule that may be extracted from them.

Imagine that the only relevant case precedent (`Godiva v. Hershey, a fictitious case`) determined that a building owner is not liable for the personal safety of people who enter the building. It could be concluded that, therefore, the landlord in the present case has no duty of care.

However, in order to build the strongest possible case for the client, compare the precedent to the present case in more detail to see how the cases may be distinguished. Imagine that in the precedent, the person who was a crime victim was loitering in the lobby of the building and was not there for business purposes.

The **issue** may then be **restated**:

```
Is a building owner liable for the personal safety of people who
enter the building for an appointment with a tenant of the
building?
```

The **rule statement** provides the elements of negligence, as well as the rule from the precedent:

```
In order to establish negligence, there must be a duty of care, a
breach of that duty, harm, and causation.
```

According to <u>Godiva v. Hershey</u>, a building owner is not liable for the safety of those who loiter in the lobby and, therefore, there is no duty of care.

E. Application

However, in the case at hand, the client entered ABC Corporation's office building solely for the purpose of doing business with one of the tenants of the building.

A duty of care must still be proven through **another rule**, such as foreseeability:

If the potential for harm was foreseeable, there is a duty of care owed by the defendant.

Then **apply** this rule to the facts:

The building owner should have foreseen that a crime such as robbery is likely to occur in an unsupervised lobby of a building because of the seclusion of a lobby from the view of passers-by on the street.

A **rule** could also be stated about the duty of building owners:

In torts and property law, building owners or occupiers have a duty of care to invitees; they owe reasonable prudence under the circumstances.

Apply this rule to the case at hand:

In this case, had the building owner exercised reasonable prudence, he would have hired a security guard for the lobby of the office building, realizing that the probability of his tenants or his tenants' clients becoming crime victims in an unsupervised lobby in an urban area was quite high.

Of course, because of the time limitations of an essay on an examination, the discussion of rules and their application might not be as extensive as they could be in a document written in legal practice.

Now that the duty of care required to prove negligence has been established, **apply** the breach and the harm elements of negligence:

The landlord, therefore, had a duty of care, which was breached because he failed to hire a security guard for the lobby of the building.

There was harm because the plaintiff was robbed.

Next, causation must be proved.

This may be done by stating the "but-for **rule**":

```
Causation may be shown by the "but-for test". In other words, if
the defendant had not been negligent, the harm to the plaintiff
would not have occurred.
```

Then **apply** this rule to the present case:

```
In this case, the building owner's failure to employ a security
guard in the lobby was the cause of the injury to the plaintiff.
The plaintiff would not have been robbed if there had been a
security guard on duty. But for the building owner's negligence,
the plaintiff would not have been robbed.
```

F. Conclusion

The **conclusion** may be stated briefly:

```
Therefore, the building owner is liable for the harm that
occurred to the plaintiff when he was robbed in the lobby after
entering the building for an appointment with one of the tenants
because the landlord had failed to employ a security guard in the
lobby.
```

Exercise VII-1:

To practice writing in the "irac" format, look up samples of Bar exam essay questions on the internet through state Bar Associations or on the website of Bar review companies. Law librarians will also be able to suggest sources of sample essay questions.

CHAPTER SEVEN-Grammar Review

Participles

1. Participles are verb forms that are used as adjectives. Present participles end in "-ing", and past participles end in "-ed".

2. The meaning of present participles is active, just as in a continuous tense from which the form is derived, generally describing the "agent" of the action. The meaning of past participles is completed action, just as in the simple past and perfect tenses, generally describing the "receiver" of the action. The meaning of the participles may also be distinguished as "cause and effect".

Examples:
```
An interesting class (The class is interesting.)
The interested students (The students are interested in the
class.)
```

Exercise VII-2:

Write pairs of sentences for each of the following. Be prepared to explain the difference in meaning of each pair.

```
Confusing/confused
Exhausting/exhausted
Amusing/amused
Mitigating/mitigated
Challenging/challenged
Growing/grown
```

N.B. Avoid the use of "dangling participles". A dangling participle is a present participle at the beginning of a sentence that does not describe the subject of the sentence.

Examples:

```
Coming home late at night, the children were already
asleep.(dangling participle-incorrect)

Coming home late at night, he found that his children were
already asleep.(participle describes subject-correct)

Taking notes, the professor lectured.(incorrect)
Taking notes, we listened to the professor's lecture.(correct)
```

CHAPTER EIGHT

WRITING A CONTRACT

I. Introduction

Although most law offices in today's world use pre-printed forms for contracts, it is important for lawyers to know how to write an effective contract without using a form. This allows lawyers to evaluate a pre-printed form and to determine whether a pre-printed form is sufficient for a given purpose. At the same time, knowing how to write a contract in English may be especially important for non-native speaking lawyers who engage in international transactions because the appropriate pre-printed forms may not always exist. Furthermore, such lawyers may need to know how to translate pre-printed forms from their first language into the language of contracts in English.

A written contract is a legal agreement when signed by both parties, and therefore, the content is the primary consideration. While the wording of a contract, so long as the meaning is unambiguous, does not affect the nature or the legality of the agreement, maintaining traditional language usage is important to maintaining a professional appearance among colleagues and clients. Moreover, if the language of a contract does not resemble that of other contracts in English, a lawyer may be concerned that some parties might question the lawyer's ability or knowledge.

II. The content of a contract

An oral contract is valid when there is mutual assent, consideration, legal competency, and a specified time period. Some contracts are required by the Statute of Frauds to be in writing in order to be valid. The Statute of Frauds was developed in England in the 17th century and may be thought of as a "Statute to Prevent Frauds."

The contracts that must be in writing to be valid include:

```
1. contracts for the sale of land or other interest in land,
2. promises based on a promise to marry,
3. an agreement by an executor of an estate to pay the debts of
   the deceased from the executor's own estate,
4. contracts whose terms state that they cannot be performed
   within one year,
5. agreements to pay the debts of another person.
```

Of course, it is advisable for all contracts to be in writing and signed by both parties.

The most vital part of a written contract is its content. A contract needs to represent all aspects of an agreement between the parties, as well as to prevent crises and protect against them as much as possible.

In writing a contract, a lawyer must imagine every problem that could arise between the parties who are entering the agreement and then provide for these possibilities in the contract. A contract, therefore, includes both terms and conditions; the terms are the points of agreement, and the conditions are the factors that may affect the terms.

Exercise VIII-1:

You are a lawyer for a construction company that has agreed to build a swimming pool for a local suburban family of two parents and two children, ages 8 and 10. The company's owner asks you to write a contract for this transaction.

In pairs, think of and write a list of as many terms and conditions as possible to which the parties should agree. Compare your lists with those of the class as a whole.

III. The language of a contract

A. Importance of language

As noted in the introduction to this chapter, it is worthwhile to become familiar with the current use of language in U.S. contracts. For non-native speaking lawyers, businesspeople, and students, developing proficiency in reading and writing contracts in English offers a challenging language exercise.

Exercise VIII-2:

Look up examples of executed contracts on the internet or in a law library.24.

Take notes on vocabulary and structural patterns.

After reading several contracts in English, what similarities do you note in vocabulary, phrases, including the wording of headings for various sections of a contract, tenses, or other aspects of sentence structure? Share examples from your notes with the class.

B. General language

The language of contracts frequently makes use of adverbs, as well as of some adjectives, that allow a contract to describe the parties and terms of the agreement very precisely. Here are some examples of such vocabulary:

```
Hereinafter, thereinafter
Heretofore, theretofore
Hereby, thereby
Hereof, thereof
Hereto, thereto
```

```
Herein, therein
Hereon, thereon
Hereunder, thereunder
Whatsoever
Aforesaid, as aforesaid
Undersigned
```

N.B. Because of the meaning of the prefixes, those words beginning with "here-", referring to a contract at hand, are used much more often in contracts than those beginning with "there-". The words beginning with "there-" in contracts would most likely be used to refer to a document other than the present contract.

Exercise VIII-3:

In pairs, write one sentence for each of the above words to which you have been assigned. Be ready to describe a possible contract context in which the words might be found.

C. Specific language

Different areas of law call for different terms in contracts. For example, the following represent possible phrases to use in a contract for the sale of an automobile.

```
The said property
For and in consideration of
To have and to hold the same unto buyers forever
True and lawful owner
The above-described vehicle
I guarantee
Free of all claims and offsets
```

Exercise VIII-4:

In pairs, write a brief contract for the sale of an automobile from one individual to another, using the above phrases.

Compare your work with the Bill of Sale for an automobile in Connecticut.24.

D. Additional contract vocabulary

Here is some additional vocabulary that is pertinent to contracts.

```
domicile, to be domiciled in
license, to be licensed in
covenant
breach of contract/to breach a contract
cure/to cure a breach
compliance/to comply with/to be in compliance with
acknowledgement/to acknowledge
```

```
Compensation/to compensate for
affiant
affidavit
disposal, to dispose of
expiry (expiration)
record, to record (also an adjective: record ownership)
inter alia (this Latin phrase usually appears in  parentheses
because it is not one of the Latin phrases that has become
incorporated into standard English, although it is widely used in
legal English.)
per, percent, per annum (these Latin words and phrases usually do
not appear in parentheses.)
express
sole (as in "sole and absolute discretion")
qualitative, quantitative
contingent upon
conditioned on
good faith
reasonable
calendar year/fiscal year
should (if)
```

Exercise VIII-5:

In pairs, write a sentence for each of the above words or phrases to which you have been assigned. Describe a possible context for each sentence.

Exercise VIII-6:

Share with the class 3-5 additional vocabulary words that you have noted that are frequently used in contracts, based on your above library or internet research of contract samples or other experience. Write a sentence for each to read to the class. Choose several examples to write on the board for the class to review and edit.

IV. Reading a contract

A. Reading to note language and structure- As we have previously noted, reading contracts will familiarize you with their use of language and thereby assist you with writing a contract.

Exercise VIII-7:

Skim the following employment contract.

1. What does "whereas" mean in the first four sections of the following employment contract?

2. What does "Now therefore…" mean, following the sections that begin with "whereas"?
3. What other structures or phrases do you note that reflect the use of language in contracts?
4. Identify 3-5 of the above vocabulary words that are found in the following contract. What is their context and meaning in the contract?

Part-time Physician Employment Agreement

This employment agreement is made as of the _day of ____,2005, by and between_____, a (state) not-for-profit corporation (hereinafter, "Employer") and _____, M.D.("Physician"), an individual domiciled and duly licensed to practice medicine in the (state of _____).

Background

Whereas, together with its affiliates, Employer has established a network of providers to satisfy the needs of the communities they serve for a range of appropriate and cost-effective health care. Employer supports this process by identifying physicians that it regards as having particular value to their communities;
Whereas, as of the commencement date of employment hereunder, Physician shall be qualified and licensed to practice medicine in (state) and be board certified in (specialty);
Whereas, the parties desire to enter into an agreement for Physician to provide his Professional Services in accordance with Employer's Bylaws, rules and regulations, and Hospital's Professional Staff Bylaws, and rules and regulations;
Whereas, the parties desire to enter into this Agreement in order to provide a full statement of their respective responsibilities in connection with the provision of Physician's Professional Services.
Now therefore, in consideration of the mutual covenants set forth herein, and intending to be legally bound, the parties agree as follows:

Terms

1. Employment-Employer hereby employs Physician to provide Physician's Professional Services as a part-time hospitalist, as described in this Agreement, and Physician hereby accepts such employment subject to the terms and conditions set forth below.
2. Conditions of Employment- As conditions of Physician's employment hereunder, Physician shall at all times:
   a. have and maintain in good standing an unrestricted license to practice medicine in (state)
   b. have and maintain a current and valid Federal Drug Enforcement Agency license
   c. be and remain board certified in (specialty)
   d. maintain participating provider status in the Medicare and Medicaid programs

e. remain in compliance with all applicable federal, state, and local laws, rules, and regulations ("applicable laws")

   f. not engage in any other employment, or in any other activity that, in Employer's reasonable judgment, interferes with the full and timely performance of Physician's duties hereunder.

3. Representations and warranties- Physician hereby represents and warrants to Employer that

   a. Physician has full right, power, and authority to execute, deliver, and perform Physician's obligations under this Agreement;

   b. the execution, delivery, and performance of this Agreement will not violate nor conflict with the terms of any order, contract, or other obligation to which Physician is a party, or by which Physician is bound.

4. Professional Services-

   a. Physician shall be available to provide Professional Services at the locations and times that Employer shall specify , after consultation with Physician, for an average of twenty-five (25) hours per week. Until specified otherwise, Physician shall provide Professional Services at the Hospital during the periods set forth on the Position Description, attached hereto.

   b. If at any time, Physician is unable to satisfy any commitment under Section 4a above, Physician shall be responsible for assisting Employer to provide or arrange for coverage by another physician ("Substitute Physician"), provided, however, that the Substitute Physician be a member of Hospital's Medical Staff.

   c. Physician acknowledges responsibility for knowing and following Hospital's standards for the completion of medical records. Physician shall include all required diagnosis and other codes thereon, and shall submit such records and documentation to Employer. Physician expressly agrees that any repeated or continuing failure to comply with the requirements of this paragraph is a material breach of the obligations hereunder and that Employer may withhold any payments that would otherwise be made to Physician until all such failures have been cured to Employer's satisfaction.

5. Other Duties- In addition to providing Professional Services as described in Section 4 above, Physician shall:

   a. participate in outreach programs to the community as reasonably requested by Employer from time to time;

   b. devote the time required or reasonably requested by Employer to administrative duties related to the operations of the Hospital;

   c. actively cooperate with the Employer in keeping controllable costs of the Hospital to a minimum, in preparing budgets for the Hospital, and in meeting the requirements of those budgets;

   d. if and when Employer determines that actual or potential patient volume would justify the placement of an additional physician or other health care provider, assist Employer to identify and recruit a qualified person and to integrate that person fully into the conduct of the Hospital;

   e. immediately notify Employer, in person or by telephone, should any of Physician's conditions of employment or representations and warranties become violated or no longer true or should any actions of professional liability be instituted against Physician, whether or not related to services performed at Hospital.

6. Annual Physician Goals and Objectives-At the initiation of this Agreement and prior to the beginning of each calendar year that this Agreement is in effect, the Chief of Physician's division and the Hospital's Chief Medical Officer (CMO), after consultation with Physician, will in their sole and absolute discretion establish a series of goals and objectives to be accomplished by Physician during the forthcoming calendar year ("Physician's Goals and Objectives"). These Physician's Goals and Objectives will focus on critical performance activities for which Physician is employed. The Physician's Goals and Objectives shall be attached to Physician's Employment Agreement.

7. Annual Review of Performance- Within sixty (60)days of the end of each calendar year, the division chief and CMO will prepare a written review of Physician's performance under the Physician's Goals and Objectives ("Annual Review"). This review will include Physician's actual performance related to the Physician's Goals and Objectives, a qualitative discussion of Physician's performance during the calendar year and an indication of areas on which Physician should work during the coming calendar year. This Annual Review will be used, among other uses and at Employer's sole and absolute discretion, in relation to Physician's Incentive Compensation (described below).

8. Employer's Duties-During the term of this Agreement, Employer shall:

   a. provide such office space, equipment, and supplies as Hospital deems needed in its sole discretion for Physician to perform the duties hereunder, it being understood that Physician shall use such space, equipment, and supplies merely to perform those duties;

   b. provide such non-physician personnel to assist Physician in the performance of duties as Hospital deems appropriate in its sole discretion after consultation with Physician.

9. Term- The term of Physician's employment hereunder shall commence on _____, 20__ ("Effective Date") and shall continue for a period of one (1) year. In the event both parties continue to perform under this Agreement after the one (1) year period has expired, the term of this Agreement shall be deemed to be continuing on a month-to-month basis, terminable by either party as of the end of any calendar month by thirty (30) days prior written notice, under the terms and conditions then applicable.

10. Termination-

   a. Upon material breach of this Agreement by either party, the party alleging the breach may provide the other party with a written description of the alleged breach, along with written notice that if the breach remains uncured for more than thirty (30) days, the Agreement will be terminated. If the alleged breach is not cured to the reasonable satisfaction of the party alleging the breach within that thirty (30) day period, the party alleging the breach may then immediately terminate the Agreement by providing written notice to the other party of the Agreement's immediate termination.

 b. Employer may terminate this Agreement immediately, or with such notice as Employer deems appropriate, upon providing written notice to Physician:

  1.) where Physician fails at any time to maintain satisfactorily any of the qualifications or requirements set forth in Sections 2 or 4 above;

  2.) where Employer determines that any of the representations and warranties that Physician made in Section 3 above were false when made or became false at any time during the term of this Agreement;

  3.) where Physician exhibits any behavior towards any patients or staff of Hospital that Employer deems grossly unprofessional; or engages in any conduct or has a personal condition that in Employer's judgment endangers patient safety; or commits any act of a kind that would be understood as to have a material adverse effect on the reputation or public standing of Employer or of Physician himself;

  4.) where Physician steals, embezzles, misappropriates, or otherwise converts any funds of Employer or affiliates;

  5.) subject to the requirements of applicable laws, where Physician is unable to perform material duties as described herein by reason of any physical, emotional, or mental condition for a total of at least ninety (90) days in any period of twelve (12) consecutive months

 c.) Either party may terminate this Agreement for any reason by providing the other party with ninety (90) days advance written notice of the intent to terminate same.

 d.) Physician agrees that upon termination of this Agreement, for any reason, Physician's medical staff privileges immediately terminate without the right to a hearing.

11. Cash Compensation-

 a. Base Salary-Physician shall receive a base annual salary of $_____ for Physician's employment hereunder.

 b. Incentive Compensation-

  1.) Employer shall provide Physician with an opportunity for a bonus based upon Physician's efforts to provide or improve the high level of care provided to Employer's patients.

  2.) Based upon the Annual Review, Physician may be eligible for a bonus of up to eighteen percent(18%) of Physician's Base Compensation paid during the prior calendar year. The actual amount will be determined by Physician's score on the Physician's Goals and Objectives ("Performance Score").

  3.) All Incentive Compensation is fully contingent upon satisfactory quality and compliance reviews. For compliance review purposes, payment of Incentive Compensation shall be conditioned on Physician's receiving a score of 95% or better on the annual compliance review performed by Employer. Should Employer in its sole discretion determine in good faith that physician has violated either the quality or compliance standards referenced in this paragraph, physician

shall be ineligible for incentive compensation during that
calendar year, and no such compensation shall be paid.
12. Benefits-
   a. Professional liability insurance-Employer shall provide
professional liability insurance coverage for professional
services rendered by Physician during the term of this
Agreement. Physician understands that this coverage will not
apply to any services that are not within the scope of his
duties for Employer as described herein.
   b. Honoraria-Physician shall be entitled to retain all
stipends and honoraria received for lectures and other
presentations.

B. Reading a contract for content

Exercise VIII-8:

1. Read the above contract in more detail. Are there any terms that may be important either to the Physician or to the Employer that have been omitted?

2. Suppose that the Employer in the above contract asks the Physician, who signed the contract, to teach a course for the Hospital. The class will meet for three hours each week. Is the Physician required to accept this assignment under the terms of the contract? If the Physician is interested in teaching the course, but wants to reduce his/her other responsibilities accordingly, does this contract allow him/her to do that?

3. The Physician has been offered a part-time teaching position at a local University. Is s/he obliged to obtain permission from the above Employer before accepting the teaching job?

4. Following his/her first year of employment, the Physician is told by the Employer that s/he will not receive any Incentive Compensation. The Physician feels that this is unfair. Does s/he have any recourse under the terms of the contract?

5. Because s/he did not receive any Incentive Compensation, the Physician wants to resign from the position effective immediately. Does this contract allow him/her to do that?

C. Reading a contract in order to advise a client

Frequently, lawyers are asked to read contracts that have been presented to clients and to advise them whether to sign them. In negotiating a contract for a client, lawyers make recommendations about inclusions or omissions in the contract that are in the best interest of clients.

Exercise VIII-9:

Turn again to the above part-time employment contract for a physician. If your client, the physician, was interested in working for the above Employer and asked you whether he should sign this contract in its present form, how would you advise him or her? Why? Are there any areas that you feel need to be negotiated or rewritten for greater clarity or fairness? Write a letter to your client with your recommendations.

D. Reading to practice comprehension/paraphrasing

Reading comprehension of contracts improves with practice.

Exercise VIII-10:

1. Read the following "Buy-Sell Agreement".
2. In one written sentence, state the purpose of the agreement. Then in one sentence, paraphrase parts I, II, and IV. Write three or four sentences to paraphrase part III.
3. Note the use of "shall". What is the difference between "may" and "shall" in a contract?
4. Note how the use of capitalization of the first letter of certain nouns in contracts differs from standard usage. Why do you suppose more capitalization is used in writing contracts?
5. How is "hereinafter" used in a contract or other legal writing? What does it tell the reader about understanding the terminology in the contract?

```
                    Buy-Sell Agreement 25.

This agreement is made this_____day of_____,20__, between
_____, a corporation of the state of_____, hereinafter
"Corporation", and _____, hereinafter "stockholders", who own
all the outstanding stock of the Corporation.

The purpose of this Agreement is 1. to provide for the sale by a
shareholder during lifetime, or by a deceased shareholder's
estate, of his interest in the Corporation, and for the purpose
of such interest by the Corporation, at a price fairly
established; and 2. to provide all or a substantial part of the
funds for the purchase.

Therefore, in consideration of the mutual promises and
obligations set forth hereafter, each party hereto agrees as
follows:
```

I. At this time, the outstanding stock of the Corporation consists of One Hundred (100) shares, and each shareholder's interest is as follows:

    _____owns fifty (50) shares
    _____owns fifty (50) shares

The Stock Certificates evidencing such shares have been or will be endorsed as follows:

"The sale or transfer of this certificate is subject to a Stock Purchase Agreement dated _____, 20___, a copy of which is on file with the Secretary of the Corporation."

While this Agreement is in effect, no shareholder shall have any right to assign, encumber, or dispose of his stock except as provided therein. The existence of the Agreement, however, shall not affect each shareholder's right to vote his stock and receive any dividends thereon until such time as he, or his personal representative, has received the purchase price for such stock, as provided herein.

II. Upon the death of the shareholder, his Estate shall sell, and the Corporation shall purchase, all of the shares of stock owned by the shareholder at the time of his death, for the price and upon the terms provided herein.

III. If a shareholder desires to sell or otherwise dispose of all or any part of his stock during his lifetime, he shall give the Corporation and each of the other shareholders written notice of his intention. If there is a prospective transferee other than the Corporation or the existing shareholder, such notice shall state the name and address of such transferees and the terms and conditions of the proposed transfer.

    Upon receipt of such written notice, the Corporation shall have the right to purchase all of the shares of stock offered for sale or transfer. The purchase price shall be the amount established in Article IV below; provided, however, that if a lower price was stated in the notice to the Corporation, it shall have the right to purchase at such lower price.

    If the Corporation fails to purchase all of the shares offered for sale within__days after receipt of the notice, the other shareholders shall have an additional ___days within which to purchase the unsold shares for the same price.

    The Corporation and the shareholders shall individually have the right to pay for any shares they purchase either in cash or upon the following terms(or upon any more favorable terms offered to a prospective transferee as stated in the written notice):____percent(_%) if the purchase price in cash upon the date of exercise of the option to purchase; the balance in equal installments evidenced by a series of ___ (__)promissory notes, the first note payable ____(__) months from the date of exercise of the option and the remaining notes payable at annual intervals thereafter, with interest at the rate of __prime plus _____(____%) per annum on each note at its maturity. Each promissory note shall include and be subject to the provisions of Article IX hereof.

    Unless the Corporation or the other shareholder purchase all of the stock offered for sale within the successive time periods allowed, upon expiry of the last such period, the stock may be disposed of to the person and upon the terms and conditions described in the notice, or to any other person or persons; provided that the notice and first offer procedure described above is repeated in connection with every other intended transfer.

Upon every sale or other disposition of an interest in the Corporation under this Article, the Secretary of the Corporation shall transfer record ownership to the new owner(s) on the books of the Corporation. Any change in the respective ownership interests of the shareholder resulting from a purchase and sale between stockholders which does not terminate this Agreement as provided in Article VIII, hereof, shall also be recorded in Schedule "A" attached hereto.

IV. At this time, the total value of the capital stock of the Corporation for the purposes of this Agreement, is $__, which is $_____ per share. This value shall remain effective for the purposes herein until there is a redetermination of value as hereinafter provided.

At the end of each fiscal year, the Corporation and the shareholders shall redetermine the value of the capital stock and shall indicate the redetermination by endorsement on Schedule "B" attached hereto, in the following form:

The total value of the stock of _as of _____, 20_, for the purposes of this Agreement, shall be $___, which is $_ per share.

Dated:_____, 20_____
Signed:_____

(The contract continues with stipulations regarding deceased shareholders.)

E. Additional contract reading practice

Here is another agreement that offers examples of the language of contracts.

Employee Confidentiality and Assignment of Inventions Agreement [26].

I understand that Multimedia Corporation, Inc. ("Company") has developed and used and will be developing and using Confidential Information in connection with its business. "Confidential Information" includes, but is not limited to, information relating to the development of interactive multimedia products such as product development and distribution plans, sources of content, licensing and royalty arrangements, profits, sales, pricing policies, operational methods, technical processes and other business affairs and methods, plans for future development and other information which is not readily available to the public. This information was developed and will be developed by Company at great expense and constitutes trade secrets of Company. To safeguard this Confidential Information, Company has instituted policies and procedures to protect such information. In connection with my employment by Company, I will come into contact with such Confidential Information.

I understand that the Confidential Information is vital to the success of Company's business and, in consideration of Company's employment policies and in consideration of Company's payment for my services, I state the following:

1. I agree that during and after my period of engagement with Company

   a. I shall keep secret all Confidential Information and not reveal or disclose it to anyone outside of Company, except with Company's written approval.

   b. I shall not make use of any of such Confidential Information for my own purposes or for the benefit of anyone other than Company; and

   c. I shall deliver promptly to Company, upon the termination of my engagement and at any time Company may so request, all software, data, memoranda, notes, records and other documents (and all copies thereof) constituting or relating to such Confidential Information which I may then possess.

2. All work which I create in connection with my engagement shall be considered to be "works made for hire" under the U.S. Copyright Act, 17 U.S.C. Sections 11101 et seq. In the event a work is not construed to be a work made for hire, I assign and will assign to Company all my rights and interests in any developments, designs, inventions, improvements, trade secrets, trademarks, copyrightable subject matter or proprietary information which I have made or conceived, or may make or conceive, either solely or jointly with others and either near or on the Company's premises, a. while providing services to Company b. with the use of the time, materials, or facilities of Company, c. relating to any product, service, or activity of Company of which I have knowledge, or d. suggested by or resulting from any work performed by or for Company (the "Developments"). I am aware that I have no proprietary interest in any Developments, including patent, copyright, and trade secret rights. Any and all inventions and other works of authorship developed by me while performing services for Company are created for and owned exclusively by Company. I further agree to provide necessary assistance to protect Company's rights and interests in such patents, copyrights, and trademarks.

I understand that this Agreement shall be governed by and construed in accordance with the laws of the state of __.

Agreed to and Accepted:
Name_____
Signature_____
Date_____

ExerciseVIII-11:

1. Timed reading: Read the above document in no more than 15-20 minutes.

Then write the answers to the following questions.

   a. What is the purpose of this agreement?

b. How would you advise a client/employee about signing such an agreement?

c. How would you advise the Company as your client? Is there anything that you would add or remove from the agreement?

2. Discuss your answers with the class.

3. In one paragraph, summarize the primary obligations of this agreement.

Exercise VIII-12:

Read the agreement again, highlighting vocabulary, phrases, and grammatical structures that you note would be useful in writing your own contracts. How does this document differ from the contracts you have read? Does this agreement include all the elements of a contract? In pairs or as a group, compare your language notes.

Exercise VIII-13:

Choose one of the following-

1. You are the lawyer for a family that owns an ice cream store. The family would like to hire a manager to take charge of the store on weekends. Imagine that they have provided you with the information that you need in order to complete the names of the parties and the terms of the agreement, and write an employment contract for the manager position.

2. Develop your own hypothetical situation, especially one that relates to your present or future law practice. Write a contract that will be important or useful to you.

CHAPTER EIGHT-Grammar Review

Articles

1. The choice of article depends on:

a. the type of noun with which it is used

The definite article (the) is used with all common nouns: singular, plural, and non-count.

The indefinite article (a,an) is used only with singular count nouns.

b. the context in which the noun is used, both the language context and the situation of the speaker and listener.

The indefinite article shows that the context does not make the noun definite, and either the speaker or listener or both do not know to what the noun refers:

```
We hope to get a dog after we finish school.

He baked a cake.
```

The definite article indicates that the noun does not have to be introduced. The speaker and listener know to what the noun refers:

```
The dog that we got after we finished school likes to take
long walks.

He baked a cake. The cake was delicious.
```

2. No article is used instead of the indefinite article (a/an) with plural count nouns and with non-count nouns:

```
They had soup for lunch. They  prepared sandwiches for
lunch.
```

Some words generally are used with no article, especially in some phrases with prepositions:

```
to go by train, on foot; at home, at school; at night; to
eat breakfast, lunch, dinner
```

Abstract and generic nouns generally do not require an article:

```
Oranges are a source of Vitamin C.

Life is good.
```

3. Additional article usage:

A/an – to classify a noun:

```
An orange is a fruit.
```

to replace "per" :

```
She walks three miles a day.
```

The- with names of geographical locations:

oceans, seas, gulfs, groups of lakes, canals, deserts, mountain ranges, groups of islands, buildings that are named

multi-word country names: `the United Kingdom`

plural country names: `the Netherlands`

multi-word proper nouns with "of":

`The University of Your City`

adjectives used as nouns:

`They were committed to helping the hungry.`

Exercise VIII-14:

Read and discuss the following information. Then discuss the grammatical use in the sentence of each of the underlined words.

`  `**`Workers' Compensation`**`-Workers' Compensation laws in `<u>`the`</u>` U.S. are designed to offer `<u>`a`</u>` compromise for `**`(why is there no article here?)`**` employers and employees. Employees `<u>`who`</u>` are injured or disabled on `<u>`the`</u>` job receive fixed monetary awards. There are also benefits for dependents of workers `<u>`who`</u>` are killed in `**`(why no article?)`**` work-related accidents or by work-related illnesses. Moreover, `<u>`the`</u>` liability of co-workers is eliminated in `<u>`most`</u>` work-related accidents. State workers' compensation statutes apply to `<u>`most`</u>` workers; federal statutes are limited to federal employees or to `<u>`those`</u>` engaged in interstate commerce. The benefit of Workers' Compensation laws to employers is `<u>`that`</u>` often `<u>`the`</u>` amount `<u>`that an`</u>` injured employee may recover is limited, while employees relinquish `<u>`their`</u>` right to sue for torts damages in `<u>`most`</u>` cases.`[27]`.`

CHAPTER NINE

WRITING A RESEARCH PAPER

I. Introduction

Research papers that are required in law school generally consist of at least 10 pages, but more usually, 20-30 double-spaced pages in length. Some elective courses require a final research paper. Others offer the choice between a final exam and a research paper. These requirements and options are usually posted with registration information so that students know of them before choosing elective classes. LLM programs usually require students to write a thesis, which is essentially the same as a research paper, although the choice of topics may be broader than those within a specific course.

II. Usage of the term "research" in law

The term "research" is used primarily in two ways in law school. Researching to prepare an office memorandum or an appellate brief means finding case precedents in order to make predictions for a supervisor or to persuade a judge about the outcome of a case. Writing a research paper, however, does not usually require researching case precedents, but rather, as in other professional disciplines, involves answering a question raised by the purpose of the research project.

For example, the topic of a research paper might be:

```
  a.)In a given international dispute, which country has the better
argument(s)?
  b.) Is a given national statute in compliance with an international
treaty?
  c.) Was a court's decision in a given case correct?
```

Although the last example may involve reading and interpreting a line of cases that influenced a court's decision, this is not the same as doing case research, which entails finding cases that relate to a case that has not yet been decided.

III. Research skills

Writing a research paper involves the same skills as writing an essay. The differences are that the paper will be longer than an essay and may consist of several combinations of rhetorical modes. Moreover, the writing will include ideas of other writers to support the paper's argument, to refute opposing arguments, or to represent opposing arguments that your paper will then refute. Information about the sources of these ideas when incorporated into your text is known as a citation. Citations may represent direct quotations or paraphrases.

If you have experience collecting sources of information for a research project in your first language, most likely the skills involved in gathering sources for a research project in English will be the same. You may have already developed a system of resource-gathering, note-taking, and outlining.

IV. Information Gathering

As you find information that pertains to your topic during the course of a semester, you may decide to keep a special notebook or a set of index cards, with one card for each citation, or you may prefer to store the information on a lap-top computer. As you note relevant readings and citations, you will begin identifying sub-topics for your paper. Make a list of these subtopics. As you find more suitable sources, arrange the information in your notes according to these subtopics.

V. Writing an outline

Write an outline for your paper according to the subtopics. When you decide that you have found sufficient information to support and develop your topic, you can begin writing. Follow your outline step by step, incorporating the information you have researched as it relates to your purpose and focus. Edit your draft for grammar and academic style. Your final revisions should combine the parts of your draft into an integral piece of writing.

VI. Preparation of citations

Keep accurate records of the sources of your citations while gathering information. You can put the citations into correct Blue-book form when you write the final draft of the paper, but in your notes, you will need to record correctly the author's name, the title and date of the publication, as well as the page number. Note the name and location of the publisher if the work is a book, and note the volume number of a journal.

VII. Final outline

When you are ready to finalize the outline of your research paper, you can review all the information you have gathered from other sources. Next to each citation, indicate the section of the paper where you will include the information. As you refine the outline, you can determine the exact purpose and placement of the citation, as well as omit those sources that are not relevant to your focus.

VIII. Writing the first draft

A. Focus

It is important to keep your focus in mind at all times as you outline and write your research paper. The more interested you are in the topic, the more you will want to read everything that you find. You may want to keep your notes on these extraneous readings, as these sources may lead you to your next research question and a future paper.

However, to write a research paper that is effective in presenting a unique perspective and in drawing persuasive conclusions, you will need to ensure that your paper includes only the information that specifically applies to your present focus.

B. Synthesis

1. introductory phrases

In order to incorporate the information you have chosen to cite into your text, phrases such as the following are often used:

```
According to (Writer X),_____
As Writer X states in his article_____,
This concept is supported by Writer X in _____
```

Cited information is often introduced by a connector:

```
In addition to Writer X's statement about _____,
Although Writer X states that _____,
However, as Writer X has shown,_____,
Therefore, according to Writer X,_____
While Writer X prefers life in a small town, s/he acknowledges
some of the advantages of living in a large city. For
example,_____
```

As you read journal articles, make notes of additional phrases and verbs that are commonly used to synthesize sources.

2. Verbs used to report information

Here are some verbs that are used to report information and that will help you avoid overuse of "said":

```
1. Verbs you can use to explain an expert's view:

describe, explain, express, find, identify, indicate, note,
observe, remind (of, about), report (on)

2. Verbs you can use to report a course of action suggested by an
expert:

advise, recommend, suggest, urge

3. Verbs you can use to show that one expert or study agrees with
another:

affirm, agree (with), concur (with), corroborate, support

4. Verbs you can use to show that disagreement exists among
experts:
```

challenge, disagree (with), dismiss, doubt, question, suspect (of), wonder (at)

5. Verbs you can use to express an expert's opinion or conclusion

argue, assert, believe, claim, conclude, determine, expound (on), maintain, propose, think

Exercise IX-1:

Practice using the above verbs by writing at least one sentence from each group that might be used to present or discuss another writer's ideas.

Exercise IX-2-synthesizing:

Imagine that you have chosen the research topic, "The Advantages of Living in a Large City" for a persuasive essay. You would like to incorporate some of the ideas presented in Essay Example C (below) to support the ideas in your own essay.

a. In pairs, identify the advantages of living in a city that Essay C presents. Using examples from the above introductory phrases, write at least three sentences that could be used to incorporate each of these ideas into your essay.

b. Identify the advantages of living in a small town that Essay C presents. Using examples from the above introductory phrases, write at least three sentences that you could use in your essay to incorporate arguments in favor of those advantages and then refute them.

Essay Example C

Life in a City or Life in a Small Town: Life is Good

Many people prefer living in a large city. Convenient public transportation, cultural and social activities, and employment opportunities attract many residents. At the same time, other people would much rather live in a small town, finding greater convenience there, as well as closer community life, and more recreational activities.

In a large city, it is possible to travel conveniently by various means of public transportation. Many urban dwellers prefer not to own a car and can then avoid the stress of driving in traffic and looking for parking places. They benefit from the health advantages of walking to the train or bus stop or to their final destinations.

People who prefer to live in large cities often cite the variety of social and cultural activities that are available and that allow them to meet friends with similar interests. They frequently attend concerts and the theater or visit museums. They also enjoy finding international fairs and restaurants that bring the whole world into close proximity.

Many city dwellers first choose to live in a large city because of the greater number of employment opportunities. They can also find highly specialized jobs, as well as a variety of settings in which to work, and a greater likelihood of jobs with flexible working hours.

In a small town, on the other hand, it is more convenient and even necessary to own a car. However, car ownership is much more convenient than in a city. There are always available parking spaces, and often the commercial area is centralized, allowing residents to complete several errands, including food shopping, without moving their cars. While the commercial areas may be farther from their house than in a city, small town residents do not usually have to contend with traffic jams.

People who live in small towns enjoy a close-knit community life that is unknown in large cities. Small town residents tend to meet their neighbors and to make themselves available to assist their neighbors when needed. Living in a small town may contribute to a sense of well-being through the sense of safety and belonging that community life inspires. Friendships in small towns are continually reinforced, as neighbors may meet each other in a variety of situations, including through their children's schools and at work.

Small town dwellers have access to recreational opportunities that also include plenty of parking. While city dwellers spend countless minutes and even hours waiting on long lines, the need to wait on line for a movie, for example, is practically non-existent in a small town. Moreover, outdoor recreational activities are usually accessible within minutes of a small town. Residents of small towns may enjoy hiking and bicycling while feeling close to nature.

In summary, there are many differences between life in a large city and life in a small town. Each one has its own characteristics and distinct advantages. Where you choose to live will depend on your individual priorities.

Exercise IX-2:

Incorporating sources into a report-

Choose a legal topic on which you would like to write a report.

Find three sources from the internet or library that you could use to develop a report on one of the topics.

Write an outline of your essay that shows where you will incorporate your sources. Include any direct quotations that you will use.

Exercise IX-3:

Write a 2-3 page report based on your above outline.

CHAPTER NINE-Grammar Review

Avoidance of 1st and 2nd persons

Generally, in academic writing, the first and second persons (I, we/you) are not used.

Exercise IX-4:

Rewrite the following sentences in a formal academic style:

1. In this paper, I would like to discuss my research on international children's rights.
2. I think analyzing an argument is challenging, and you will probably agree, so we will discuss whether the majority or the dissent had the better argument in this case.
3. You can never be sure of a person by their words alone; you need to observe their actions, as well.
4. My conclusion is that vampires still exist.
5. I have found many examples of this to prove my point.

Articles and Quantifiers

Quantifiers are used with count and non-count nouns to indicate a non-specific amount.

With singular count nouns-

```
Each, every
```
N.B. The meaning of "each" is each individual item in a group, while the meaning of "every" focuses on the total items in the group and is similar in meaning to "all", except that "all" requires a plural verb.

> **Examples:** Each textbook is individually priced.
> Every textbook is of the highest quality.

With plural count nouns-

```
Many, a great many, a number of, quite a few, several, few
```

With non-count nouns-

```
Much, not much, a great deal of, a large/small amount of, little,
a little, not much, any, no, none of
```

With both-

```
All, most, a lot of, plenty of, some/any, enough, hardly any, not
```

N.B. When the indefinite article is used with "little" or "few", indicating an amount exists (there is at least some), the meaning is positive. When "little" or "few" is used with no article, the meaning is negative, focusing on the absence of a quantity.

Examples:

Don't worry. They have a little money.

They cannot make a donation right now because they have little money.

We have a little time. We can still get to the theater in time for the first show.

We have little time. We will not arrive on time.

Exercise IX-5:

As a group, decide whether to choose the topic, "The Meaning of Criminal Justice", or another legal or current events topic with which everyone is familiar.

In pairs, take turns writing sentences about the chosen topic, using as many quantifiers as possible within a pre-determined time limit (for example, 10-15 minutes).

_____

CHAPTER TEN

EDITING

I. Grammar/writing/editing activity: quotations

A. Discuss the following quotations in pairs or small groups, if possible. Then each pair or small group chooses a reporter to summarize the discussion for the class. The class may decide to continue the discussion through questions or comments.

B. Write a timed paragraph (20-30 minutes) in class in which you react to one of the quotations.

```
1. The guilt of a government is the crime of a whole country.
Thomas Paine(1737-1809) journalist during the U.S. Revolutionary War. 28.

2. It is impossible to calculate the moral mischief that mental
lying has produced in society. When a man has so far corrupted
and prostituted the chastity of his mind as to subscribe his
professional belief to things he does not believe, he has
prepared himself for the commission of every other crime.
Thomas Paine. 29.

3.All, too, will bear in mind this sacred principle, that though
the will of the majority is in all cases to prevail, that will,
to be rightful, must be reasonable; that the minority possess
their equal rights, which equal laws must protect, and to violate
which would be oppression. Thomas Jefferson (1743-1826), writer of the
Declaration of Independence, Third U.S. President, in his First Inaugural Address,
March 4, 1801. 30.

4. Democracy is two wolves and a lamb voting on what to have for
lunch. Liberty is a well-armed lamb contesting the vote.
Benjamin Franklin (1706-1790), journalist, scientist, a writer of the U.S.
Constitution, U.S. ambassador to France. 31 .
```

C. In pairs, exchange paragraphs. Circle the areas about which you have grammar suggestions or questions. Discuss these areas, identify the grammar involved, and then explain the appropriate grammar and correct structure to the class.

II. Discussion/writing/editing activity: the right to bear arms

In pairs or small groups, discuss quotation #4 above.
Set a time limit for the discussion (20-30 minutes, for example).
Choose a reporter to take notes about your discussion.
In your discussion, consider the following questions:

A. The U.S. Constitution's Bill of Rights includes "the right to bear arms." 32. The colonists felt strongly about obtaining this right because prior to the Revolutionary War, only the British were allowed to be armed. British soldiers had also been allowed to enter and occupy the homes of colonists. In your opinion, does the historic context support any important reasons to allow private citizens to own guns today?

B. What is your opinion about gun control? Should there be laws that prohibit private citizens from owning guns? What is your reaction to the argument today of those who oppose gun control: "if guns are outlawed, only outlaws will have guns"?

C. Are private citizens allowed to own guns in your country? If not, do you think that gun control or the absence of it in your country has any effect on the crime rate?

D. Discuss any additional perspectives that you may have on this topic.

E. At the end of the discussion, the small group reporters will present their summaries to the class. The class may offer questions or comments for further discussion.

F. Write a reaction to the quotation and/or to your group's discussion, either as a timed writing exercise, or as a homework assignment.

G. In pairs, exchange essays before giving them to the instructor. Share your editing suggestions about any aspect of the essay: grammar, paragraph or essay structure, focus, etc. Be sure to give positive feedback, as well.

III. Discussion –instructor's corrections

Review the notations and suggestions by your instructor on all of your corrected essays, making sure that you understand and agree with them. Raise any questions about them that you may have in class, or share a grammar point with the class from your corrected work if you feel it might be useful for discussion, even after it is clear to you.

IV. Student Presentation - grammar activity

In pairs, for homework, choose an area of grammar to present to the class. Design a spoken or written exercise or activity for the class based on this area of grammar. Be prepared to lead the class activity and to answer any questions that may arise about the area of grammar you have chosen.

V. Editing practice- punctuation

Add appropriate punctuation, including capitalization, to the following passages.

A.

The Statute of Frauds

The statute of frauds began in england in 1677 its purpose is to prevent fraud by requiring certain kinds of contracts to be in writing in order to be enforceable the most important examples of such agreements are an agreement for the sale of land or any other interest in land an agreement whose terms state that it cannot be performed within one year from its inception an agreement by an executor of an estate to pay the debts of the deceased from the estate of the executor a contract to pay the debt of another person in the u.s. each state has adapted the statute of frauds which is a defense in other words the statute of frauds can be used by those accused of fraud if there is no written agreement and the agreement is included in the statute of frauds even if the contract is of a kind that does not need to be in writing to be enforceable it is still advisable to put all contracts in writing for example when a contract is assigned to someone other than one of the original contracting parties it will be easier to enforce that contract if it is in writing

B.

Evidence: Exceptions to the Hearsay Exclusionary Rule

"the supreme irony of the hearsay doctrine is that a vast amount of hearsay is admissible at common law and under the federal rules the full analysis of any hearsay problem therefore requires considering whether the offered evidence is hearsay and then if it is hearsay whether any exception to the rule of exclusion applies to it
" the exceptions give special treatment to recurring instances of hearsay…the federal rules also provide for admission of hearsay as part of an experts testimony even if no specific hearsay provisions would allow it so long as the material is of a type usually relied upon by such experts
" some types of hearsay are thought to be particularly free from the risk that the maker of the statement intended to lie statements of this kind are usually admissible whether or not the declarant is available to testify other types of hearsay are thought to be particularly necessary in special circumstances these types of statements are usually admissible only if the proponent shows that the declarant is unavailable finally there is a third class of out-of-court statements offered to prove the truth of what they assert that universally is allowed into evidence despite the hearsay rule even without a belief that the statement is likely to have been truthful when made or that the statement is particularly necessary to a party's case this class of statements includes admissions which are any statements ever made by a *party* in the current case if introduced against that party and certain statements made out of court by a person who appears in court as a *witness…*" [33].

VI. Editing practice-grammar

Correct the grammatical errors in Essay Example E, which follows. Change the structures to formal ones where necessary. Assume that the paragraph and essay structure are correct.

Essay Example E (persuasion)

```
                   Life is Better in the City

     Sometimes you will hear people say, "That's life in the big city"
to mean that life is not always fair or easy. This saying, however,
gives an impression of the value of city living that in itself is
unfair, in my opinion. Living in a city has many advantages that living
in a small town cannot begin to compare with. These include
opportunities for professional development and promotion, cultural and
intellectual activities, as well as people to share them with, and
experiencing cultural diversity that makes it possible to learn first-
hand about other parts of the world without having to travel.

     First, professional opportunities abound in a large city. Not
only there are institutes and Universities that offer continuing
education classes, you can also enroll in a degree program without
commuting very far from your home or workplace. Moreover, by continuing
your education, you will improve your chances for promotion in your
present job. Or it is also possible to discover a new interest that may
become a hobby or even a future career.

     In addition to such intellectual stimulation, there is also many
possibilities for artistic stimulation through museums, galleries, and
concert halls. In many cities, the architecture itself surrounds us in
art, history, and spirituality. Such cultural experiences remind us
that people are capable after all of empathy, of creating beauty, and
of sensitivity and insight. It is uplifting to the spirit to remind
these human qualities. It reminds us to look for what is good and what
is beautiful in each person. It can motivate us to decide what is truly
important in life and to reflect on spiritual matters such as our
purpose for living.

     Finally, the diversity of people in a large city can teach us
about other ways of life in other countries. Through international
exhibits, craft sales, folk dancing, and restaurants, a city can become
a microcosm of the world that city dwellers can learn from and enjoy on
a daily basis. In fact, city dwellers have the opportunity to
participate in an effort to build greater harmony through these
exchanges with other cultures and the way they contribute to
understanding of international world-views.

     In conclusion, living in a city has many advantages that is not
available in small towns. Educational and professional opportunities,
as well as cultural and international activities, make the quality of
life in a city both stimulating and a reward. That's life in the big
city.
```

CHAPTER TEN-Reference Information

1. Self-Editing in Academic Writing Checklist- usages to avoid

2. Correction Symbols

3. Correction Table

4. Websites for Students and Practitioners

5. Verbs and Adjectives Plus Prepositions

6. Phrasal Verbs and Possible Synonyms

7. Verbs Plus Gerunds or Infinitives

8. Irregular Verbs

Self-Editing in Academic Writing Checklist-usages to avoid:

1. conjunctions (and, but, so) at the beginning of a sentence (informal)
2. use of first or second person (I, we, you) (informal)
3. use of "going to" to express the future tense (informal)
4. use of all progressive tenses (informal)
5. slang or colloquial expressions, unless they are in quotation marks (informal)
6. use of hyphens for punctuation (informal)
7. overuse of the verb "to be" (use of a more precise and active verb is preferable)
8. overuse of "said" (redundant, and not so precise as other verbs for reporting)
9. use of the verb "to get" (informal)
10. ending a sentence with a preposition (informal)
11. "splitting" an infinitive or separating "to" from the base form of its verb (informal)
12. phrasal verbs (informal)
13. unclear use of "it", "this", or "that" (the preceding noun or concept to which these refer should be clear)
14. "run-on sentences" (generally, those with more than two-three clauses)
15. incorrect punctuation
16. incorrect subject-verb agreement
17. incomplete sentences (sentence fragments)
18. incorrect use of tenses
19. non-parallel structure
20. incorrect preposition following a verb or adjective
21. incorrect use of gerund or infinitive after a verb
22. use of pronoun before a gerund (use a possessive pronoun)
23. erroneous use of non-count nouns or quantifiers
24. "dangling participles"
25. incorrect punctuation of essential or non-essential clauses

Correction Symbols

a	article problem
adj	incorrect adjective
adv	incorrect adverb
cap	incorrect capitalization
coh	coherence of paragraph
cncs	be more concise
dm	dangling modifier
d	diction (slang, offensive or sexist language)
det	use concrete details
dev	inadequate development
frag	sentence fragment
ger/inf	incorrect use of gerund or infinitive
infrml	informal
n-count	count or non-count noun
org	paragraph not organized
p	punctuation error
possv	use a possessive before a gerund
prep	incorrect preposition
quant	incorrect quantifier
ref	unclear or incorrect pronoun reference
rep	needless repetition
run-on	run-on sentence
shft	inappropriate shift in topic or perspective
sp	error in spelling
s-v	faulty subject-verb agreement
t	tense
thesis	thesis unclear or unstated
v	vague
var	lack of variety
vocab	word choice
//	lack of parallel structure
^	insert something
P	new paragraph
No P	no paragraph
inv	invert something
?	meaning unclear
>	indent

Correction Table

Assignment Correction Symbol	#1	#2	#3	#4	#5	#6	#7	#8	#9	#10
a										
adj										
adv										
cap										
coh										
cncs										
dm										
d										
det										
dev										
frag										
ger/inf										
infrml										
n-count										
org										
p										
possv										
prep										
quant										
ref										
rep										
run-on										
shft										
sp										
s-v										
t										
thesis										
v										
var										
vocab										
//										
^										
P										
no P										
inv										
?										
>										

Websites for students and practitioners

The following websites may be of interest to you as a law student or practicing attorney. The list is by no means intended to be comprehensive. Please make any suggestions in class for additions that you may have.

www.law.cornell.edu

```
-Legal Information Institute (LII)
-includes cases, Constitutions, codes
```

www.supremecourtus.gov

```
-U.S. Supreme Court website
-includes syllabi and opinions of recent U.S. Supreme Court cases and
texts of oral arguments
```

www.usinfo.state.gov

```
-U.S.  State Department information
-includes the current political conditions of countries
```

www.oyez.org

```
-Since 1995, a non-profit, educational website about the U.S. Supreme
Court
-includes audio of oral arguments, written summaries of cases,
questions related to the issues of cases on the docket
```

www.abanet.org

```
-American Bar Association website
-includes information about current cases and other events in a variety
of areas of law
-includes many subsections related to legal specialties (for example,
abanet.org/child)
```

www.whitehouse.gov/news/releases

www.deathpenaltyinfo.org

www.nlj.com

```
-National Law Journal website
-Free temporary subscriptions available
```

www.bna.com

-Bureau of National Affairs website
-includes coverage of legal and regulatory developments for professionals in business

www.findlaw.com

-includes cases, "boiler plate" forms, actual contracts

www.uslegalforms.com

-includes sample forms for contracts

www.aclu.org

-American Civil Liberties Union website
-Founded in 1920, the ACLU's purpose is to conserve individual rights guaranteed by the Constitution

www.landmarkcases.org

-discussion of the issues and holdings of famous U.S. cases

www.dol.gov

-U.S. Department of Labor website

www.echr.coe.int/Eng/judgments.htm

-European Court of Human Rights
-includes texts of decisions

www.world.lii.org

-World Law Information Institute website
-includes decisions of the European Court of Human Rights

www.npr.com

-National Public Radio website
-includes audio and texts of their broadcasts of interviews and discussions on current topics
-NPR is supported by contributions from listeners, not by advertisers.

www.cnn.com

-CNN news website

Connectors

Logical Connectors

1. **simple addition**- also, in addition, furthermore, moreover
2. **emphatic addition**- what is more, as well, besides
3. **intensifying addition**- in fact, as a matter of fact, actually
4. **alternative (other possibility)**- on the other hand, alternatively
5. **introduction of an example**- for example, for instance, to illustrate, as an example
6. **important or the most important examples**- especially, in particular
7. **identification of what has been mentioned or implied**- namely, specifically
8. **clarification or rephrasing of what has already been mentioned**- that is, in other words
9. **show of similarity**-similarly, likewise, in the same way
10. **show of contrast**-however, in contrast, on the other hand, though
11. **contradiction of previous statement**- in fact, however
12. **reservation without contradicting previous claims**-even so, nevertheless, despite (this), in spite of (this), on the other hand
13. **result**- as a result, because of, due to, consequently, therefore, thus, hence
14. **purpose**- in order to, with this in mind, for this purpose

Sequential Connectors

A. Chronological

1. **beginning**- at first
2. **continuation**- eventually, subsequently
3. **conclusion**- at last, in the end

B. Chronological and Logical

1. **beginning**- first, first of all
2. **continuation**- next, then
3. **conclusion**- finally, last

C. Logical

1. **beginning**- the first (+ noun), one (+ noun)
2. **continuation**- second, the second (third, etc.) + noun, a second (third, etc.) + noun
3. **conclusion**- the last + noun, a final + noun, to conclude, in conclusion

Verbs and Adjectives Plus Prepositions

Here is a list of some frequently used verbs and adjectives and the appropriate preposition that is used with these words. Please note that these combinations are not the same as phrasal verbs because the meaning of these verbs does not change when the preposition is added. Therefore, this list represents grammatical structures that are appropriate for formal writing. Phrasal verbs, on the other hand, are considered to be informal.

Verbs **Adjectives**

Verbs	Adjectives
To agree with	To be absent from
To apologize for	To be accused of
To apply to, for	To be acquainted with
To approve of	To be associated with
To argue with, about	To be aware of
To believe in	To be capable of
To blame for	To be committed to
To care about, for	To be concerned about
To compare with, to	To be content with
To complain about, of	To be convinced of
To consist of	To be dedicated to
To contribute to	To be divorced from
To count on	To be engaged to, in
To decide on	To be equipped with
To depend on	To be excited about
To discriminate against	To be exhausted from
To distinguish between, from	To be exposed to
To dream of, about	To be faithful to
To escape from	To be familiar with
To excel in	To be finished with
To excuse for	To be fond of
To feel like	To be friendly to, with
To fight for	To be frightened by
To forget about	To be furnished with
To forgive for	To be gone from

Verbs and Adjectives plus Prepositions (continued)

Verbs	Adjectives
To hide from	To be grateful to, for
To hope for	To be guilty of (to feel guilty for)
To insist on	To be innocent of
To introduce to	To be interested in
To keep (prevent) from	To be involved in, with
To look forward to	To be limited to
To object to	To be located in
To participate in	To be made of, from
To pray for	To be married to
To prevent from	To be opposed to
To prohibit from	To be patient with
To provide with	To be pleased with
To recover from	To be polite to
To rely on	To be prepared for
To rescue from	To be protected from
To respond to	To be proud of
To stare at	To be qualified for
To stop from	To be related to
To subscribe to	To be relevant to
To substitute for	To be remembered for
To succeed in	To be responsible for
To take advantage of	To be satisfied with
To take care of	To be tired of, from
To thank for	To be used to
To think about, of	To be worried about

Phrasal Verbs and Possible Synonyms

To bring about	to cause
To bring up	to rear (children), to mention (topic)
To call back	to return a phone call
To call off	to cancel
To call on	to ask someone to speak in class, to visit
To call up	to call on the phone
To catch up (with, on)	to reach the same point
To check into	to investigate, to register at a hotel
To check out of	to leave a hotel
To cheer up	to encourage
To come across	to find or meet by chance
To do over	to do again
To drop in on	to visit without a formal invitation
To drop off	to leave at a place
To figure out	to solve
To fill out	to complete (an application)
To find out	to discover
To get along with	to relate well to someone
To get back	to return, to receive again
To get off	to leave a plane, bus, train
To get on	to enter a plane, bus, train
To get out of	to leave a car, to find a way to avoid
To get over	to recover
To get through	to finish
To get up	to arise
To give back	to return
To give up	to stop trying
To go over	to review
To grow up	to become an adult
To hand in	to submit an assignment in class
To hang up	to end a phone conversation, to put clothes on a hangar
To have on	to wear
To keep out of	not to enter
To kick out of	to force someone to leave
To look into	to investigate
To look out for	to be careful
To look over	to review
To look up	to search for information
To make up	to invent, to compensate for an absence or missed work
To name after	to give a baby the name of another person
To pass away	to die
To pass out	to distribute, to lose consciousness
To pick out	to select
To pick up	to take someone by car, to take in one's hand

To point out	to indicate
To put away	to remove to an appropriate place
To put back	to return to the original place
To put off	to postpone
To put on	to put clothes on one's body, to dress
To put out	to extinguish

Phrasal Verbs (continued)

To put up with	to tolerate
To run into	to meet by chance
To run out of	to finish a supply
To show up	to appear
To shut off	to stop a water faucet, machine, light
To take after	to resemble
To take off	to remove, to leave
To take over	to take control
To take up	to begin a new hobby
To tear down	to demolish
To think over	to consider carefully
To throw away	to discard
To try on	to put on clothing to check the fit or look
To turn down	to lower the volume, to decline an invitation
To turn in	to submit an assignment, to go to bed
To turn off	to stop a water faucet, machine, light
To turn on	to begin a faucet, machine, light
To turn out	to stop a light
To turn up	to increase the volume

Verbs Plus Gerunds or Infinitives

Please note that the verbs marked with an asterisk may be followed by either a gerund or an infinitive.(Structures with neither a gerund nor infinitive may also be possible.)

Verbs marked with two asterisks may be followed by either a gerund or an infinitive, but the meaning will change depending on whether an infinitive or a gerund is used.

Verbs + Gerunds	Verbs + Infinitives	Verbs+Noun+Infinitive
To admit	To afford	To advise*
To advise*	To agree	To allow
To anticipate	To appear	To ask
To appreciate	To arrange	To cause
To avoid	To ask	To challenge
To begin*	To begin*	To convince
To complete	To care	To dare
To consider	To claim	To encourage
To continue	To consent	To expect
To dare	To continue**	To forbid
To delay	To decide	To force
To deny	To demand	To hire
To discuss	To deserve	To instruct
To dislike	To expect	To invite
To enjoy	To forget**	To need
To finish	To hesitate	To order
To forget**	To hope	To permit
To keep (continue)	To intend	To persuade
To like*	To learn	To remind
To love*	To like*	To require
To miss	To love*	To teach
To postpone	To manage	To tell
To practice	To need	To urge
To prefer*	To offer	To want
To recall	To plan	To warn
To recommend	To prefer*	
To regret**	To prepare	
To remember**	To pretend	
To risk	To promise	
To start*	To refuse	
To stop*	To regret**	
To suggest	To remember**	
To tolerate	To seem	
To try**	To start*	
	To struggle	
	To swear	
	To threaten	
	To try*	
	To volunteer	
	To wait	
	To want	
	To wish	

Irregular Verbs

base form	simple past	past participle
Be	was/were	been
Bear	bore	borne/born
Become	became	become
Begin	began	begun
Bend	bent	bent
Bind	bound	bound
Bite	bit	bitten
Bleed	bled	bled
Blow	blew	blown
Break	broke	broken
Bring	brought	brought
Broadcast	broadcast	broadcast
Build	built	built
Buy	bought	bought
Catch	caught	caught
Choose	chose	chosen
Cling	clung	clung
Come	came	come
Cost	cost	cost
Creep	crept	crept
Cut	cut	cut
Deal	dealt	dealt
Dig	dug	dug
Do	did	done
Draw	drew	drawn
Eat	ate	eaten
Fall	fell	fallen
Feed	fed	fed
Fight	fought	fought
Find	found	found
Flee	fled	fled
Fling	flung	flung
Fly	flew	flown
Forbid	forbade	forbidden
Forecast	forecast	forecast
Forget	forgot	forgotten
Forgive	forgave	forgiven
Forsake	forsook	forsaken
Freeze	froze	frozen
Get	got	gotten/got
Give	gave	given
Go	went	gone
Grind	ground	ground
Grow	grew	grown
Hang	hung	hung
Have	had	had
Hear	heard	heard
Hide	hid	hidden
Hit	hit	hit
Hold	held	held

Hurt	hurt	hurt
Keep	kept	kept
Kneel	kneeled/knelt	kneeled/knelt
Know	knew	known
Lay	laid	laid
Lead	led	led
Leap	leaped/leapt	leaped/leapt
Leave	left	left
Lend	lent	lent
Let	let	let
Lie	lay	lain
Light	lighted/lit	lighted/lit
Lose	lost	lost
Make	made	made
Mean	meant	meant
Meet	met	met
Mislay	mislaid	mislaid
Mistake	mistook	mistaken
Pay	paid	paid
Put	put	put
Read	read	read
Ride	rode	ridden
Ring	rang	rung
Rise	rose	risen
Run	ran	run
Say	said	said
See	saw	seen
Seek	sought	sought
Sell	sold	sold
Send	sent	sent
Set	set	set
Shake	shook	shaken
Shed	shed	shed
Shine	shone/shined	shone/shined
Show	showed	shown
Shrink	shrank/shrunk	shrunk
Shut	shut	shut
Sing	sang	sung
Sit	sat	sat
Sleep	slept	slept
Slide	slid	slid
Speak	spoke	spoken
Speed	sped/speeded	sped/speeded
Spend	spent	spent
Spin	spun	spun
Spit	spit/spat	spit/spat
Spring	sprang/sprung	sprung
Stand	stood	stood
Steal	stole	stolen
Stick	stuck	stuck
Sting	stung	stung
Stink	stank/stunk	stunk
Strike	struck	struck/stricken
Strive	strove/strived	striven/strived
String	strung	strung
Swear	swore	sworn

Sweep	swept	swept
Swim	swam	swum
Swing	swung	swung
Take	took	taken
Teach	taught	taught
Tear	tore	torn
Tell	told	told
Think	thought	thought
Throw	threw	thrown
Thrust	thrust	thrust
Understand	understood	understood
Undertake	undertook	undertaken
Upset	upset	upset
Wake	woke/waked	woken/waked
Wear	wore	worn
Weave	wove	woven
Weep	wept	wept
Win	won	won
Wind	wound	wound
Withdraw	withdrew	withdrawn
Write	wrote	written

N.B. The verb "to lay" is transitive, while the verb "to lie" is intransitive. Keeping this grammatical distinction in mind can help avoid misuse of these verbs and their past tense and participial forms.

End Notes

1. See www.quotationspage.com
2. The Bluebook: a Uniform System of Citation (Harvard Law Review Association et al. eds., 17th ed.2000).
3. Id.
4. Stumbling Towards Sustainability (John C. Dernbach, ed. 2002) at 5.
5. Id. at 47.
6. Id. at 47.
7. Lewis Solomon & Alan Palmiter, Corporations (1999) at 7-8.
8. Abraham Maslow, Towards a Psychology of Being (1968).
9. George Fletcher, Basic Concepts of Legal Thought (1996) at 32-33.
10. See www.oyez.org for a discussion of the facts, issue, and holding of Marbury v. Madison.
11. Maslow, supra note 8.
12. Berne Convention for the Protection of Literary and Artistic Works, July 24, 1971, Statutory Supplement to Cases on Copyright (Brown & Denicola, eds. 2002) at 275.
13. The Copyright Act of 1976, id. at 18.
14. Solomon & Palmiter, supra note 7 at 3
15. Id. at 4
16. Id. at 4.
17. Id. at 5.
18. Id. at 8-9.
19. Id. 9-10.
20. Id. at 199-200.
21. Id. at 201.
22. Id. at 202.
23. Id. at 203.
24. Miranda v. Arizona, 384 U.S. 436 (1966). In this case, the U.S. Supreme Court found that the police practice of interrogating individuals without notifying them of their Constitutional rights violated the Fifth Amendment. Police in the U.S. are currently required to give crime suspects the "Miranda warnings", i.e., to tell them that they have the right to remain silent, the right to an attorney , and that anything they say may be used against them in a court of law.
25. See www.uslegalforms.com
26. See wwwluslegalforms.com
27. For more information regarding labor law in the U.S., see the Law Information Institute website, www.law.cornell.edu, and the U.S. Department of Labor websire, www.dol.gov.
28. See www.quotationspage.com
29. Id.
30. Id.
31. Id.
32. U.S. Constitution , Amendment II.
33. Arthur Best, Evidence (Aspen Law & Business 2001) at 89-90.

ORDER INFORMATION

To order additional copies of Legal Writing for International Students, please

contact the publisher:

Peconic Press
P.O. Box 370631
West Hartford, CT. 06137
www.peconicpress.com

email: info@peconicpress.com

Thank you for your interest.